AUTHENTIC LIVES

To Willi and James,
    With gratitude for your
ministry in FMBS and as
                    teachers!
my

AUTHENTIC LIVES

Blessings,

OVERCOMING THE PROBLEM OF HIDDEN IDENTITY
IN OUTREACH TO RESTRICTIVE NATIONS

THOMAS HALE III

26. 05. 2018

WILLIAM CAREY
LIBRARY

Published by William Carey Library
1605 E. Elizabeth St.
Pasadena, CA 91104 | www.missionbooks.org

Melissa Hughes, editor
Sharon Edwards, copyeditor
Joanne Leong, graphic design
Rose Lee-Norman, indexer

William Carey Library is a ministry of
Frontier Ventures | www.frontierventures.org
Printed in the United States of America

20 19 18 17 16   5 4 3 2 1 BP300

Library of Congress Cataloging-in-Publication Data
Names: Hale, Thomas, III, 1965- author.
Title: Authentic lives : overcoming the problem of hidden identity in outreach to restrictive nations / Thomas Hale III.
Description: Pasadena, CA : William Carey Library, 2016. | Includes bibliographical references and index.
Identifiers: LCCN 2016034783 (print) | LCCN 2016035386 (ebook) | ISBN 9780878086344 (pbk.) | ISBN 087808634X (pbk.) | ISBN 9780878088973 (ebook)
Subjects: LCSH: Missions. | Identity (Psychology)--Religious aspects--Christianity.
Classification: LCC BV2063 .H24 2016 (print) | LCC BV2063 (ebook) | DDC 266--dc23
LC record available at https://lccn.loc.gov/2016034783

"The first to present his case seems right, till another comes forward and questions him."

Proverbs 18:17

CONTENTS

ACKNOWLEDGMENTS

Many thanks to friends, family and colleagues who encouraged me to write this book and helped me write it by contributing ideas, improvements and corrections. Without you it would not have been possible. I am also indebted to the libraries where I researched and wrote. I found a treasure trove of helpful information, especially via inter-library loan.

Thanks to my parents for a place to live during the final write-up and to my wife and sons for supporting me in this task.

Thanks also to Jeff Minard and staff at William Carey Library. Jeff, you and your team have been great to work with and your encouragement has meant a lot. Sharon Edwards' copyedits have made this a much better book. Thank you! Wendy Hayes, Melissa Hicks, and Melissa Hughes guided me well through the process of getting the book published.

May this work bring insight and resolution to those who struggle with the hidden-identity approach.

THE PROBLEM OF HIDDEN IDENTITY

Let me take you on a journey. Our destination, which I call Almoria, is not just one place but a composite of dozens of countries in the Middle East, North Africa, Asia, and the former Soviet Union. The people we will meet there—and the stories we will hear—are a mix of hundreds of people's experiences from these places. The following dialogue is also composed from many real conversations.

"So you know James, do you?" Alex asked. "It all sounds very interesting, what's happening there in Almoria, to judge from his letters. But one thing bothers me."

"What's that?"

Alex is a faithful friend and supporter of James, and I was curious to know what was bothering him.

"Why do we have to be so careful about what we write to him?" he said with a slight frown.

"Surely you know that letters might get opened by postal officials there," I replied.

"Yes, but why the secrecy? He was sent there by a missionary organization—I contributed to his financial support. Why can't I write to him about that?"

"Well, you know he isn't a *missionary* there. He's teaching computer science."

"But his real purpose is to share the gospel, isn't it? At least that's the way the organization's literature describes it."

"Does it? Well, that may be his private purpose, but he can't publicly describe himself that way," I explained. "Even if the authorities in Almoria are aware of a missionary purpose—and they probably know everything they want to know about him—he can't make it public or they'd have to expel him."

"Why is that?"

"Because the Almorians don't want missionaries. They think missionaries will undermine their families, their culture, and possibly even their government! It isn't true, of course, but few Almorians know that. Not many know that missionaries are people of goodwill. So if James were publicly described as a missionary, the authorities would have to do something. But if his private purposes are kept private, then there's no problem. They don't lose face that way."

Alex looked clearly surprised. "Don't his activities cause a problem?"

"No, because he never preaches in public and he fulfills his role as a teacher to the best of his ability and with full professionalism. So there is no problem from his activities."

"I don't know." The skepticism was evident in his tone and expression. "It still seems too much like a secret agent story to me."

"Times have changed, Alex," I said quietly. "Many countries don't grant missionary visas, or else they put lots of restrictions on missionaries. In order to live long term in a 'restricted-access' country like Almoria, you can't go as a missionary. You have to go with another profession. Some people call it 'creative access.'"

"Well, I guess things *have* changed. Maybe James does have to hide his missionary identity when he's in Almoria." Alex paused for a moment before adding, "But I still don't like that approach!"

DEFINING THE PROBLEM:
THE TENSION OF HIDDEN IDENTITY

Anyone called to a restrictive country like Almoria faces the tension of having to assume a hidden identity, for very rarely can one go to these places with a public identity of "missionary." Today, more than seventy countries are as restrictive as our fictional Almoria, up from thirty-eight in 1978.[1] And many of the restrictive countries go farther than Almoria in curtailing missionary activity.

Some followers of Jesus have suggested that avoiding the designation "missionary" would resolve the tension of identity. But even if no finances are involved, the fact of being sent makes a person a missionary. You may not think of yourself as a missionary, but a "sent one" is a missionary. Some definitions specify the sender or the mission, others do not. Regardless, when it comes down to it, being sent with a call from God is what makes one a missionary. If God has called you to Almoria, then you are in fact *sent*, whether or not any other people were involved in the sending. The fact that you know you were sent by God makes you a missionary, just the same as if you had been sent by a church. Whether or not you call yourself a missionary is another question, which will be addressed later. So the only way "not to be a missionary" is to end up in Almoria completely apart from any sense of being called there.

How then can someone called by God to Almoria fulfill that calling? If a calling from God makes one a missionary, and Almoria does not welcome missionaries, what can one do? Most sent ones have resolved this dilemma by hiding their missionary identities and living with the tension created by keeping their sending a secret. This approach is the one adopted by almost all sending organizations today. But as we will see, the hidden identity creates a number of problems. Unless you feel completely at ease living with a secret, you will struggle with a hidden identity. You may feel more like a secret agent than a sent one of Jesus. You may find that your definition of honesty is stretched to the limit.

---

1. As Larry Sharp asserts, "More than seventy countries of the world, representing about sixty percent of the world's population, do not grant visas for missionaries" (2012:480). Compare that to the 1978 figure of thirty-eight countries that "permit no foreign missionaries of any type or greatly restrict any evangelists within their own countries" (Wilson 1980:144, citing Ed Dayton of World Vision's MARC, *MARC Newsletter*. Monrovia, CA: World Vision, September 1978).

Fortunately, at least one other option is available: modify the mission so that you can be sent openly. This approach creates its own tensions, and some will prefer to stick with the hidden-identity approach in spite of its problems. Neither approach is completely free of tensions, but I argue that the tensions inherent in the "modified-mission" approach are preferable to those in the hidden-identity approach. Modifying a mission requires us to take a fresh look at the way we say things. Take "reaching the lost," for example: how does that sound if you are the one being referred to as "lost?" Unless you share the same conception of "lostness," you might well be offended.

What if we were to speak instead about *loving* people? Love certainly includes a concern for someone's eternal destiny and their closeness to God, but it also includes much more. Love values the whole person. Love is a motivation that will not lead us astray.

Speaking about love instead of lostness is just one way to suitably modify our mission. Whatever way we choose, what is important is to reexamine and reevaluate our mission in light of both Scripture and the current context in Almoria. As we internalize our modified mission and "own" it, we make it a part of our "core identity," to use Rick Love's term (2008:34). This identity includes our vocation *as a key part*—not simply as a way to enable "real" ministry in some other sphere of life.

Let us look now at an example of the tension created by a hidden identity. Jayna felt called by God to go to Almoria for long-term service. She knew that Almoria requires missionaries to register with the government and lets them stay only one year. Jayna was an engineer and was called to work as an engineer, not as a religious worker. She was, however, a member of a sending organization registered in her home country as a missionary organization. She struggled with whether to present only engineering as her reason to be in Almoria, or to tell the full story.

Jayna felt it was legitimate not to consider herself a missionary; she knew that most expatriate followers of Jesus working in places like Almoria do not use that word. But she also had heard that Almorian officials would place her in the missionary category if they knew of her membership in the sending organization. Furthermore, her desire to tell others about Jesus could place her in the category of missionary.

She could try to "stay under the radar" by avoiding certain public activities or unnecessary publication of her role as a sent one. That way, even if the secret police knew she was a missionary, there would be no particular reason why they would need to take action against her since her missionary status would not be apparent to others.

Jayna was troubled by the fact that all of her options relied on withholding or bending the truth at some level. She had been told by her leaders that it was justified. Some felt that the government of Almoria was wrong to limit religious freedom, wrong to require registration. Others argued that the government's categories were wrong because they implied that a foreign believer whose faith takes any public form other than participating in public worship is a missionary. Jayna remained unconvinced by these arguments. She wondered if she should either be registered as a missionary, whatever the consequences for her duration of stay, or else resign from the sending organization to avoid having a hidden identity.

In some cases, a hidden identity can be kept hidden, even if a person's story is publicized. This was true of Sung Han, an expatriate worker who was killed in Almoria; his identity was not compromised even in the publicity that followed. There were different accounts of why he was killed. Some said it was simply robbery, others said it was because he had Almori copies of the *Jesus* film. Sung Han's organization correctly maintained that he had not been proselytizing, and this was paraphrased in the media as "he was not a missionary." Yet, in at least two supporting churches, Sung Han was listed as just that: a missionary. This was not publicized, so it remained a hidden identity.

In a different case, both the "development" identity and the missionary identity became widely known. Two American women were kidnapped in Asia in 2001. After they were released, they gave a television reporter their identity as aid workers, but a prayer card describing them as mission workers was also broadcast. As Rick Love, former international director of a sending organization, puts it, "their two worlds collided." Love notes that "the same could have easily happened to many other agencies and cross-cultural disciple makers" (2008:34). It is not always possible to keep an identity hidden.

In other cases, it is not a matter of whether or not an identity remains hidden, but rather a question of how the act of hiding or the need to do so impacts local relationships. Phil, an expatriate follower of Jesus who ran a business in Almoria, found himself in an awkward situation with one of his employees. The company's staff included other expatriate believers like Phil, as well as Almorian citizens of various faiths or no faith. As the business grew, Phil needed an assistant to help manage the ten departments. Some of his colleagues advised him to hire only a believer, but there was no qualified believing candidate available. Phil promoted Radan, an employee from a different faith, to the position, choosing not to discuss other expatriates' faith-based aims with Radan. This may have worked from a business perspective, but Radan's beliefs prevented Phil from being completely at ease with him. How could Phil have avoided this situation? Maybe he could have found a believer to hire instead of Radan. Or maybe he could have been more open with Radan. Phil was aware of these options, but he felt that the hidden identity of the expatriates was the source of the problem.

Kevin found himself in a different sort of awkward situation, in a moderately restrictive country where he could get a visa as a religious worker, but could renew it only for a limited number of years. His final renewal was about to expire, so his local boss— the leader of a Christian institution—suggested that he not apply for a religious visa, but request a visa through a charitable organization. He could do development work for them once a week and consultation on an ad hoc basis. His main work, though, would remain at the Christian institution. Kevin followed his leader's advice, seeing it as local wisdom, but he wondered where to draw the line between wisdom and deception.

No doubt some see the hidden-identity approach as the *only* option other than giving up altogether. Many would argue that having a hidden identity is normal, even acceptable. Jesus taught us to be as shrewd as snakes, not just as innocent as doves (Matt 10:16), and he did much of his teaching in parables, which many listeners did not understand. Numerous other biblical examples also support the "shrewd as snakes" approach. In 1 Samuel 16:2–3, for example, God himself tells Samuel to declare (and fulfill) a purpose other than his primary purpose when he goes to anoint David as the next king of Israel.

A distinction must be made here between hidden identities and hidden agendas. In the story of David's anointing, Samuel's *identity* as prophet of God is never in question; it is his *purpose* of king-making that is concealed. Anointing David was definitely a hidden agenda of Samuel's but he had *no* hidden identity. In the pages that follow, we will touch on hidden agendas here and there, but the focus will be on hidden identity. An agenda can be *part* of one's identity, and a hidden agenda is something most have experienced—whether their own or someone else's. A hidden *identity*, however, is less common—something we associate with spies or terrorists, not with followers of Jesus.

Not that a hidden agenda is normally associated with followers of Jesus either! It has too negative a connotation. For this reason, I will speak of "private purposes" when the matter arises, not of "hidden agendas." But since hidden agendas—by whatever name—are more common than hidden identities, we are better placed to deal with them. As a friend of mine likes to say, "Everyone has an agenda. So why shouldn't I have one, whether or not I publicize it?" And if I am praying for opportunities to share Christ with people,

I am certainly not obliged to publicize that; one's prayer life is private (Matt 6:6).

Returning to identity, each of us has multiple identities connected to our different roles in family, community, work, and church. We are under no obligation to disclose every one of them in each location. But even though disclosure of every identity in every situation is not required, it does not mean that carrying the burden of a hidden identity is a good thing.

Some readers may remain unconvinced that there is a problem with the hidden-identity approach to serving God in Almoria. But listening attentively to those who have struggled with this approach might persuade them otherwise. It is not easy to remain at peace while holding secrets, and it may sometimes mar one's testimony or integrity. Withholding information is also a questionable example to set, particularly if one works in a culture that already suffers from lack of transparency. In the rest of this book, I will present further reasons why a different approach would be better, but for much of the book I simply accept as valid the concerns that have been expressed to me about the hidden-identity approach. Even if it were only a question of addressing the needs of those sent ones who feel uncomfortable with keeping secrets, it would be enough reason for change. It is not acceptable to dismiss their concerns by simply telling them to have more faith and to carry on. It is for these reasons that this book has been written. Finally, although the primary focus in the book is on the importance of the means as well as the end result, we need to ask ourselves, "How effective is the hidden-identity approach in achieving its ends?" I and others are convinced that it has not been effective in reaching its goals. Even if that were an overstatement, the changes proposed in this book would not harm results and might in fact improve them.

A much better option than a hidden identity is an integrated identity, the same for all audiences. This is especially true in relation to social media, on which contacts from different arenas of one's life can all see each other. Unless one plans to somehow hide them from each other (which may or may not be technically possible), an integrated identity is a must. To have one identity for all audiences, however, requires a changed approach on the part of those serving in Almoria: it means giving up the treasured title of "missionary" in home churches. It means bringing the *churches*, not just the sending organizations, to a new understanding of outreach. The current understanding of outreach comes from a context that no longer exists. No longer do Christians wield decisive political power in dominant nations and no longer do those nations hold the same kind of power over other peoples that they did a century ago. These changes have profound implications for the outreach of the church both at home and abroad, yet because Christians have been so used to their position in the world, few have changed the way they view their outreach.

I am not a theologian or a Bible scholar, nor am I a professional historian, and this book may not bring any churches to a new understanding of outreach. It may, however, encourage those expatriate followers of Jesus in Almoria who have struggled with the problem of a hidden identity. It may challenge leaders of organizations and professors of missiology or church mission pastors to rethink the suitability of hidden identity as a strategy for outreach. It may give new ideas to those considering service in another culture, ways that they can fulfill their calling without taking on a "missionary" identity that must not be disclosed. And it can help friends in the country of origin to better understand the issues faced by those whom they help go to Almoria. It is my hope that this book will lead readers to examine themselves and their approaches. It may even lead churches to give equal status to *all* their members, rather than a higher status to those who "live by faith" in that they are fully-supported workers. Just as much faith (and maybe more) is needed to find or create "real" jobs in the difficult places, keep them, and shine a light through them.

I am a follower of Jesus who has lived as a guest in foreign countries most of my life. For more than twenty years, I have seen fellow expatriate followers of Jesus struggling with the problem of a hidden identity. This book came into being as I wrestled with that problem beginning in 2008 and became convinced that someone should work through the related issues carefully and rigorously. Dozens of fellow expatriate followers of Jesus, living in places like Almoria, have encouraged me to write this book.[2] They are looking for a way to serve God in their restrictive contexts without having to keep secrets.

I grew up in Nepal, where my parents were missionary doctors for twenty-five years. They had a clear identity as missionaries living with certain restrictions, carefully worked out with the government by the founders of the United Mission to Nepal. When I myself went to work in the former Soviet Union shortly after its breakup, I did not go as a missionary but as an English teacher. I could be an English teacher and also a follower of Jesus who affirms with Acts 4:12 that "salvation is found in no one else," who wants everyone in the world to know and experience that saving work. This, of course, requires that people hear the message of Jesus; but although people hear from those who are sent, those who are sent need not bear the title "missionary." As we will see, "missionary" has too many false negative connotations for continued use.

NAMES, TERMS, AND DEFINITIONS

I have used the fictitious Almoria for a number of reasons. The incidents and stories told in this book took place in a variety of countries and contexts, but putting them in Almoria allows me to write as if they all happened in a single country. The name Almoria also replaces "the country you are called to" simply because that phrase is too awkward to use repeatedly. Similarly, "the Almori

---

2. My opinions do not necessarily reflect the views of all of these people, or of the organizations in which I have worked or the institutions at which I have studied. I have therefore omitted any mention of my organizational and institutional affiliations.

people" takes the place of more general references to ethnic groups that restrict the religious freedom of their people.

At some points in the book I use the adjective "Almori," and at others "Almorian." I realize it might have been easier for some readers had I eliminated one or the other term. However, I chose to use both because, in a majority of countries, the distinction is a significant one. The "Almori" people are a particular ethnic group within Almoria. They have given the country their name but they are not its only ethnic group. Other citizens of Almoria are not referred to as Almoris but as Almorians. Because Almoris are distinct from other Almorians and have a different status and in some cases different rights, it is appropriate to keep that distinction by the use of "Almori" when referring to the specific "titular" ethnic group and "Almorian" when referring more generally to citizens of Almoria.

A further reason for the use of a fictitious country is also the reason for changing names and identities of individuals in the vignettes and stories throughout the book. I have also altered other details of the stories so as to protect people's privacy. Even though I seek to avoid secrets myself, I cannot make that choice for others. I am committed to respecting their privacy. My concern for others' privacy also led me to omit a detailed history of the development of the hidden-identity approach because doing so would inevitably reveal details that could create difficulty for others.

A word is needed about the term "hidden-identity approach" as opposed to "creative access." Some go so far as to call creative access "deceptive access," yet that is only true if there is a hidden identity. Creative access can include many different ways of being in Almoria, with or without hidden identity. I do not use the term "creative access," however, because it too often serves as a euphemism for the hidden-identity approach. It will be clear that my suggestions for improvement relate to the hidden-identity approach, not to creative access in general.

One of the main reasons for the hidden-identity approach is the strong negative connotation of "missionary" and other terms. We saw this in the conversation with Alex at the start of the introduction. Outside the church, the connotations of "missionary" are too negative for its continued use. For many Almorians, "missionary" conveys the idea of paying individuals to change their religious affiliation; such a change is seen as a betrayal of one's people and one's family. Other Almorians suspect "missionaries" of being agents of a foreign power who aim to destabilize Almoria by creating inter-religious tensions. "Missionary" also carries an implied set of activities: full-time preaching or proclamation, or perhaps church work or seminary teaching. Never mind that in its Latin derivation *missionary* simply means "one who is sent." Although the term "missionary" may convey a high status within churches that send missionaries, it conveys pariah status among those who are opposed to them. Why should sent ones suffer simply for the word "missionary?"

Since there is nothing sacred about the designation of "missionary," there is no essential reason for continuing its use. Other words are also avoided by expatriate followers of Jesus in Almoria, words such as "evangelism," "church planting," and "conversion." These terms too have unhelpful negative connotations. Even the word "Christian" has too many extra meanings in today's world. In the former Soviet Union, for example, "Christian" implies a nominal Russian Orthodoxy, so it does not often convey the meaning it does for evangelicals: someone who has made a personal commitment to follow Jesus as Lord and Savior.

Because of the negative connotations of traditional terms, I use alternative terms with minimal negative connotations whenever possible. "Christian" and "missionary" are replaced with "follower of Jesus" and "intercultural worker" or "sent one." Exceptions occur when the less loaded terms sound too awkward, when "Christian" or "missionary" is the only word that fits the context, or when the traditional terms occur in quotations from other authors. Another change in terminology is from "cross-cultural" to "intercultural," whether referring to outreach or to those engaged in the outreach. *Cross-cultural* carries an implication that the ones doing the crossing have all the answers; *intercultural* reflects the more accurate picture that learning happens in both directions.

As for definitions, I deliberately refrain from defining intercultural outreach. Numerous definitions have already been proposed, and heated debates have been (and continue to be) held about them. I neither add my own definition to the list nor take sides in the debate. The problems of a hidden-identity approach apply to all definitions that include proclamation of any sort and a geographical scope that encompasses restrictive countries. As for other terms, they are explained when they first appear in the text.

OVERVIEW

Some might feel that my concerns about hidden identity are overblown. Chapter 2 presents my reasons in detail. Nevertheless, for many of the questions discussed in this book, there is no single "right" answer; the answer depends on the context, on individual gifts and callings, and even on personality. Numerous books and organizations project the premise that their approach is *the* correct approach, and that all others should adopt it. In writing this book, I call readers to decide for themselves and to refrain from judging others. A careful look at history—and at the Bible—suggests that God uses many different approaches to accomplish his purposes, even our mistakes or approaches that we later see to have been flawed. Having said that, I am not suggesting that we repeat what were clearly mistakes or deliberately continue using flawed methods. How absurd would that be!

To say that the hidden-identity approach leaves much to be desired is not to suggest that workers with a hidden identity have done something wrong. Withholding information is not normally a crime. It is partly a matter of personality and gifting: some people are more reserved than others. They are naturally more able to keep things to themselves than the extroverted types. There are also times and seasons for everything. For those called to live long term in Almoria, with a primary calling other than evangelist or preacher or literature distributor, there is simply no need for all the stratagems or secrecy. They can find a livelihood that is financed in ways that need not be hidden and simply be who they are, wherever they are. It may not be easy to find this livelihood, and it may be less comfortable and secure than a livelihood earned via a sending organization, but it can be done.

Hidden identity *can* be replaced by a core identity that is the same for all audiences. Part I of this book consists of two chapters that examine various issues related to core identity for intercultural outreach. Chapter 1 sets out a basic identity of "guest" for all expatriates and examines the relationship between guests and hosts in restrictive countries. It discusses various reasons why many governments oppose intercultural outreach by followers of Jesus, and suggests a balanced, biblical response to that opposition. Chapter 2 looks in detail at the problems of a hidden identity, including the way in which deliberate withholding of information affects one's witness and one's person. This chapter also explains the concept of core identity, an understanding of oneself and one's purpose that allows for consistent transparency in any context. Core identity includes not only one's identity as a follower of Jesus, but also one's vocation. Vocation is not just something we do, it is a part of who we are. Chapter 2 closes with a discussion of the need to modify our mission and the metaphors we use to describe it.

Part II contains three chapters that suggest ways for the ideas of Part I to be implemented in practice, taking into account the needs and concerns of both current practitioners and newly recruited workers of all ages and stages of life. Chapter 3 looks at the process of finding a modified mission, including the need for careful research prior to starting a new venture. Chapter 4 addresses the problem of finances: old models may no longer be appropriate or successful. Chapter 5 looks at issues of non-financial support, such as accountability and fellowship, and suggests sources that some readers may not have considered.

The two chapters of Part III, which are of a more academic nature, come at the end of the book because this is not an academic work and these chapters may be of less interest (though not of lesser importance) to non-academic readers. They are included as chapters rather than appendices because the changes suggested in Parts I and II will be difficult to implement unless one shares at least some of the convictions presented in Part III. These final chapters provide the theological and philosophical basis for the rest of the book. Chapter 6 discusses two conceptual areas that have contributed to the development of the hidden-identity approach: ancient and recent historical legacy, and our understanding of ethics. Chapter 7 offers a brief biblical framework for God's people to serve interculturally without hidden identities. It focuses particularly on the value of all the gifts and the importance of service in all areas of life, not just those areas that have traditionally been considered "spiritual."

STEPS FOR ACTION, REFLECTION, AND GROUP DISCUSSION

1. Do you agree that the hidden-identity approach creates unnecessary problems? Which of the problems seems most pertinent to you?

2. How would your actions be different if your goal in outreach changed from "reaching the lost" to simply "loving people"? Make some of these changes in the days ahead.

3. Does a "fully-supported" role in a sending organization take more faith than getting and holding a "regular job"? How can you live by faith, whatever your source of income may be?

4. Do you object to finding new terms to replace words like missionary, evangelism, church planting, conversion, and even Christian? If so, can you find any biblical requirement for the continued use of these terms? Note that the name "Christian" was given to followers of Jesus by non-believers, not by themselves (Acts 11:26, 26:28; 1 Pet 4:16).

PART
ONE

HIDDEN IDENTITY VERSUS INTEGRATED IDENTITY

CHAPTER ONE

GOVERNMENTS AND THEIR GUESTS

Even an ambassador is only a guest.

We now consider more fully the reasons behind Almoria's attitude to and restriction of missionaries. As we will see, it is not only sent ones who are targeted, but other foreigners as well. We will then look at a biblical response to government opposition or restrictions.

EXPATRIATES ARE ALWAYS GUESTS

One source of difficulties is that too many expatriates have a wrong attitude concerning their role in Almoria. They easily forget that as foreigners they are guests in the country they have entered. Even an ambassador is only a guest.

In today's world, a visa stipulates some of the conditions for the invitation. We must never lose the perspective of ourselves as guests, unless we actually obtain citizenship in our adopted country. Bernard Adeney, author of a seminal work on intercultural ethics, puts it this way: "One of the worst things a guest can do is to take away the rights of a host to be the host" (1995:132). In other words, if we as foreigners have become so much at home and so much in control that we are running the show, we have taken away the host's position as host. Perhaps this is one of the tensions for those who have served in a particular place over decades: it becomes harder to act like a guest and to be perceived as a guest. Some Almorians might be tempted to ask, "Why doesn't this guest know when it is time to leave?" For some expatriates, there will be a time to transition from guest to permanent resident or even citizen; we will discuss that in Chapter 3, but for now we will treat all expatriates as guests.

The Kyrgyz people, who have a rich tradition of hospitality, have a saying that expresses their expectations of a guest. Expatriates in any country would do well to heed this ancient wisdom. The saying goes: *"Konok koidon josh,"* meaning, "A guest is quieter than a sheep." The implication is that guests should not tell hosts how to run their household. Visitors with "all the answers" may find this a hard injunction to follow. They should work on their listening skills and withhold their answers until they have understood the local situation better.

The Bible does not give specific instructions about how we are to act as good guests—probably because the concept of a guest was well understood by people in biblical times. It did not need to be explained or stated. Nomadic culture is closer to biblical cultures than Western cultures are, so the authors of the Bible no doubt would have agreed with the Kyrgyz proverb above. A few biblical passages obliquely touch on the role of a guest, but only one of them gives useful information about guests in the context of the passage. This passage is Genesis 18, where three "men" (v. 2) visit Abraham.

As *The Expositor's Bible Commentary* notes, "In opening the narrative with the statement that the Lord 'appeared' to Abraham, the author leaves no doubt that in some (albeit unexplained) way the three men represented the Lord's appearance to Abraham" (Sailhamer 1990:142). Abraham immediately insists that they stay for food (vv. 3–5); in doing so, he is being a proper host. The three men wait while he arranges for the meal (vv. 6–8). Only after he brings it do they say anything to him at all, and their first order of business is to give a blessing: the promise of a son (v. 10). They do later confront Abraham and Sarah about her laughing response to the promise (vv. 13–15). At the very end, after some internal debate (vv. 17–19), God tells Abraham what will happen to Sodom and Gomorrah (vv. 20–21). Abraham then engages in his famous dialogue with God about how many righteous people it would take to save the cities from destruction (vv. 23–33).

Woven into this passage, we see that even God follows the protocol for a guest in this instance. But not all guests are good guests, as we shall see.

THE TROUBLE WITH GUESTS

Even a good guest may bring unwanted change to his or her hosts: any interaction with people from different backgrounds brings that possibility. Newcomers may influence us in ways we did not expect. Change can be positive or negative, but in general cultures tend to be conservative and view most change negatively. Even when we want change, we want it on our own terms, in our own way. Guests, however, often bring change and new ideas on their terms. These changes may be cultural changes or changes to the structure of power and authority.

When people follow Jesus they will bring change to their culture; sent ones should do their best to ensure that these changes come from following Jesus and not from following the foreign culture of the sent one. It is next to impossible for sent ones to keep their own culture or worldview out of their message entirely. And whether a sent one does well or poorly at keeping the message pure, culture change may be puzzling and at times even painful for those in the midst of it. We need to understand this and be sensitive to this dynamic as it affects the Almorian government's position regarding foreigners. I came to this conclusion when new "freedom of religion" laws were introduced in various former Soviet countries in the years before 2010. These laws drastically reduced the religious freedom that had been enjoyed by former Soviet citizens after the breakup of the USSR. I did not support the laws, but I sought to understand the thinking and the concerns behind them. One of the concerns had to do with culture change.

Even though culture change is a concern of Almorian authorities, foreign guests are not the sole agents of culture change.
Change is a part of life, even for cultures that attempt to isolate
themselves. It can come through the media or through food or
clothing imports. Many countries have a love-hate relationship
with American television and movies, for example. Their people
may enjoy watching them, but the dominance of American popular
culture is often seen as an invasion. Even such supposedly neutral
parts of a foreign culture as sports or food can wear away at local
culture. On various occasions, French farmers have protested against
McDonald's, and American sports are on the whole less successful
internationally than the English sports of cricket and soccer. While
baseball and basketball may have noticeable "footprints" across the
globe, American football clearly does not.

Religious change—to the extent that it is a worldview change
and not just a change of rituals—goes to the deepest levels of a
culture. For this reason, evangelism, conversion, and church
planting raise objections from leaders of any group being targeted.
Furthermore, evangelism is perceived as arrogant, evoking questions
of this nature: *How can you assert that you are the only ones who have
truth?* Conversion feels like betrayal by the convert of his or her
people and family. Church planting feels as though cells of foreign
agents are being established.

Such changes might be tolerated if it were just a question of
one person sharing what is important to him or her. But anything
that smacks of unfair advantage will surely create opposition. And
missionaries, whether they are paid professionals or organized volunteers with special training, are seen as having an unfair advantage
in a conflict of cultures. On a more surface level of culture, one of
the reasons American culture is often resented is this sense of unfair
advantage over local expressions. The economic power and military
might of the United States make it difficult for other cultures to
hold their own.

Culture change can be brought by any stranger, even by people who do not think they are bringing it. This may explain the vicious response to aid workers sometimes exhibited by militants in the Middle East or Central Asia. When one recognizes that aid workers are inevitably bringing culture change as well as aid, then the militants' response is easier to comprehend. Expatriate foreign language teachers can be particularly active change agents, because they necessarily include cultural matters—including values—in their lessons. New learners need this cultural information in order to use their new language appropriately. But teachers would do well to carefully consider the impact that their culture lessons could have on the local culture. At the level of values, a Western teacher is likely to put a strong positive spin on the individualism found in Western cultures; for example, a teacher might encourage students to pursue their own dreams regardless of their family's approval or disapproval—an action that could have a huge negative impact on those families. At the level of cultural matters, a teacher needs to be careful about how to present holidays. If students from a conservative culture that separates young men and women start to celebrate Valentine's Day, for example, that could also draw a hostile reaction from their elders.

In his book *Under Solomon's Throne*, anthropologist Morgan Liu describes a situation where outside values entered a society through a foreign volunteer. A young Central Asian woman from a traditional family gets to know an American Peace Corps worker in her town. The woman's new acquaintance, writes Liu, "influenced her ideas about independence from her family." The American considered this a good trait, whereas the Central Asian family felt quite the opposite about it. The young woman, for her part, "resented the control her father sought to exert on her movements" (2012:122). Was the father's control an appropriate protection for a young woman or simply a manifestation of patriarchal oppression? The answer is not as simple as it may seem, because either choice has profound implications for society, and each choice has its drawbacks. The point is that the very presence of a foreigner encouraged the young woman to pursue her desire for independence from her family. That desire may have been there in any case, and one can certainly make an argument for its legitimacy. But the presence of a foreigner dramatically changes the balance in the situation, a change rarely welcomed by conservative members of the society.

Some of the cultural values Westerners hold dear—but which others may not appreciate—are individual freedom, the democratic process for choosing leaders, the importance of taking initiative to improve one's situation, and the refusal to accept a status quo that is less than it could be. Introducing these values may cause as many shockwaves in a non-Western culture as the introduction of foreign religious beliefs.

To better understand why cultural change is unwelcome, let us conduct a thought experiment. As far as it may be from reality, let us imagine for our experiment that the world is upside down: instead of being the world superpower, the U.S. has splintered into a dozen independent entities. Most of them are impoverished and struggling with instability. In contrast, the Middle East is the dominant power bloc, and an organization based there is offering development consultants to the needy mountainous country of Appalachia. The consultants are all Muslim and along with their expertise, they are seeking to spread their faith. No doubt some Appalachians care little about any faith, and are merely grateful for the consultants' aid. Others, faith aside, may reject all aid because it hurts their pride to receive it. Still others, aware of the stated or unstated religious aims, may prefer to forego assistance rather than risk any conversions to Islam. A similar range of responses exists today in Almoria. A thought experiment like this helps us to *love our neighbors as ourselves* by making us more aware of how it feels to be on the receiving end of assistance that comes with cultural or religious strings attached.

Some expatriates take the matter of their cultural influence more seriously than others. In one small Central Asian city, a foreign couple wanted to join the local Baptist church. They knew that the

Baptists were particularly conservative, and so they met with the leader of the group and told him of their desire to join. He asked about their background and they did not hide the fact that their previous church background was not as conservative. The leader felt uncomfortable about asking them not to join, and so he extended an invitation, but with a condition: the foreign couple must not bring cultural influences into the church. The couple had expected such a reply and in the end chose not to join the church. They knew it would be impossible to have no influence. They also knew that expatriates can unknowingly (and sometimes knowingly) foster divisions in local churches, both by introducing new ideas and new ways and by enabling those already discontented to step out in new directions. And this couple refused to be the cause of such divisions.

One cultural trait that is often brought into Almoria by sent ones is the tendency to be project-oriented rather than person-oriented. Somewhat surprisingly, this is often true even when the expatriates come from people-oriented cultures. Being project-oriented means that other people's interests take second place to the accomplishment of our goals, whether the goal is to start a church or to establish a profit-making company. Our lives speak louder than our words, and people can tell if we are spending time with them because of friendship or because they will help us reach our goals.

In some cultures, building a strong relationship is actually an essential part of reaching other goals. A friend told me the story of an American businessman who flew to an oil-rich country to conclude a contract with an Arab counterpart. The American hired a lawyer with experience in the region, but disregarded his advice to spend time hunting and socializing with his host, activities that were completely unrelated to the contract. The extra time would have necessitated extending his trip and postponing other engagements at home. No doubt the businessman considered socializing with his counterpart a waste of time, but the Arab interpreted his refusal to spend that time with him as a lack of interest in the relationship (which it was), and therefore refused to sign the contract or continue discussions. For him, a good personal relationship was an essential foundation for the business project.

Unlike the commercial objectives of an oil tycoon, the projects organized by followers of Jesus are focused on the people whom they can benefit, or those who may come to faith in Jesus. But it does not matter that the goal may be "for their good" or even for their eternal salvation. If people feel they are valued only for what they can contribute to a project, they will not be interested in our project, however beneficial it might be for them. This is often true even of those who may be paid to work on the project: they may be grateful for the income but not committed to the project unless they feel the leaders are committed to them as individuals.

Sometimes one has to lay aside a project in order to focus on an individual. Lauren, a worker in Almoria, related how she specifically did *not* invite a certain neighbor to the events organized by her team for proclamation purposes. Lauren wanted her neighbor to know Jesus, but she valued her as a person and somehow intuitively felt that the "event" approach did the opposite. So instead of inviting this neighbor to the events, Lauren gave her frequent invitations to her home. The end result of those conversations may never be known, but there can be little doubt that the neighbor was receptive to what she heard from Lauren at her home. This is not to suggest doing away with all evangelistic events (though in more and more contexts such an approach is simply not possible), but rather to emphasize the importance of genuine relationships.

Adeney summarizes some of the factors that lead us to under-value relationships:

> Evangelicals want to defend the faith and convert
> the lost. Therefore they are defensive and feel
> victimized for their faith when they are not accepted.
> Since they understand the gospel in abstract terms
> as a message that must be accepted, they easily slip
> into a professional-client relationship with local
> people. They have a product that they must sell to

the locals. Even with the best of intentions, they separate themselves from the people they came to serve. (1995:51)

Instead of focusing on a product to sell (however wonderful the product in question), Adeney joins with theologian and anthropologist Anthony Gittins in calling sent ones to take the role of strangers and guests. As such, they can avoid the two extremes that come from seeing oneself as the one who should be in control: one extreme keeps sent ones from receiving anything from their hosts ("What do they have that we would want?"), and the other leads to making demands of the hosts ("Do they want our help, or don't they?"). What would happen if expatriates, in the role of guests, focused on relationships instead of on building their own projects?

But foreigners can pose a threat to more than just Almori culture: they may also be perceived as a threat to Almori leaders or authorities, including church leaders. Many expatriates come to a country with a church-planting agenda or with a particular theological perspective that is new to the local church. In a place where no church exists among a particular people group, a case can be made for one being started by expatriates. But all too often, in a place and people where there already are churches, promising young leaders-in-training leave their local church to join an expatriate. This desertion is not entirely the fault of the expatriate; often the ones who left the local church were being stifled by over-controlling senior leadership, or by a theology that the expatriates would consider extreme and unbalanced. But is a church split God's prescription for those problems? Sometimes splits result in greater church growth in the long run, but that shows only that God works all things for good, not that God loves church splits! Surely there are better ways to bring growth than by sowing disunity.

Money also plays a role in moving junior-level Almorian leaders out of their current work, unless expatriates are thoroughly committed to cooperation with local efforts rather than competition or duplication. Expatriates are usually better funded than Almorians, and can hire away the most gifted people. This hurts the Almorian entity even if no divisions arise out of the departure of the young leader in question. And as if the drain of talented leaders were not enough, expatriate endeavors may also duplicate preexisting local efforts. Such duplication is often a poor use of resources, and it regularly results in friction and competition with local entities.

All of this does *not* mean that expatriate workers should never have gone to Almoria in the first place or that they are disobeying God by staying. God's purposes are bigger than we can understand, and he uses even hurt and duplication and division in his own way. Nevertheless, this truth about God does not permit us to knowingly continue practices that hurt our brothers and sisters. Just because God can use our mistakes to build his kingdom does not mean we should continue making them. We are seeking first *God's* kingdom, after all, not our own.

Most governments are not concerned about what happens in churches. The authorities may in fact be pleased by division among believers. But when authorities are trying to control religious groups tightly, they may seek to force unification of disparate groups. In the Soviet Union, for example, government insistence on having only one evangelical group to deal with led to Pentecostals joining the Union of Evangelical Christians/Baptists, which had been created by the merger of other denominations in 1944. The resulting hierarchical structure "was imposed by the Soviet authorities as a means of controlling the church" (Rowe 1990:185).

The point of these examples of expatriates causing problems in churches is that *the same kinds of things happen to any other national entity* when faced with foreign money or foreign know-how. If expatriates are wealthier and more powerful, or are citizens of an influential country, they are likely to dominate joint efforts with Almorians. Too often, the assumption of the foreigner is: "I know best what needs to be done." This attitude easily creeps into work done by expatriates, whether they are from the West or from the East. Our societies have been successful, and it is only natural to think that what worked for us will work for others as well. That assumption ignores context and culture—and we foreigners rarely understand local culture well.

Is it really true that because our countries are wealthier or "more advanced" everything is better done our way? Professor of Islamic Studies Carl Ernst writes of "an intoxicating sense of superiority" we may feel because our culture is identified "with advanced science and technology." He uses an example which is already well out of date, but if one substitutes a commonplace device of today for a VCR, the statement still holds: "Even those of us who find it difficult to program a VCR still consider ourselves the proprietary owners of modern science" (2003:200). Perhaps the situation in our country of origin is indeed better than the situation in Almoria. This state of affairs is unlikely to be the case in *all* areas of life, but let us assume that it is. Even so, to simply transfer methods from my country and expect them to produce the same results in Almoria is unrealistic. Almoria is a totally different context. But because foreigners usually control the purse strings, their way most often prevails in spite of the fact that it might not actually be best for Almoria.

Even initiatives that most Almorians would agree are good may be perceived as troublesome by government officials. If officials have abused their power, for example, they may fear exposure by aid workers. People with a mission often speak out against injustice.[3] If aid work is not viewed as troublesome, it may nevertheless be seen as irrelevant: not everyone agrees about what is good for society, and relief and development aid has a mixed record by any honest assessment.[4]

---

3. I include "secular missionaries" here even though they would fiercely resist being called that. But in fact, those who go abroad preaching the message of human rights are just as much missionaries as those preaching a religion. They do not form churches, but they do seek to form or support civil-society organizations to promote their causes.

4. For a scholarly argument about the problems of development aid, see *Despite Good Intentions: Why Development Assistance to the Third World Has*

Lukewarm response to the introduction of family medicine in Central Asia is an example of foreign aid being misunderstood or considered largely irrelevant. As long as aid money was paying for the retraining of doctors and for family-medicine residency programs, cooperation was forthcoming. But a closer look revealed that the retrained doctors were continuing to practice in their former specialties of pediatrics, internal medicine, or obstetrics/gynecology. They had not understood the point of family medicine. Or perhaps they had understood it perfectly but had rejected it as a foreign imposition unnecessary in their context. The truth is probably somewhere in between. What is certain is that local doctors expressed ambivalence toward the foreign program.

Ambivalence toward foreigners has a political dimension. During the late colonial period, missionaries generally enjoyed the support of colonial authorities.[5] This official standing may have helped them obtain access to various communities, but the connection with colonial officials meant that in the eyes of many national leaders they were seen as the ideological arm of colonial power. At the end of the colonial period, newly independent nations often considered missionaries not only as a threat to their traditional religions but also as agents of colonialism. Secular aid organizations have also been seen by recipients of their assistance as agents of foreign governments, working to fulfill their governments' agendas.

In regard to suspicion of missionaries and aid workers, it is helpful to consider the following definition of a crime: "any offence

---

Failed by Thomas W. Dichter (Amherst, MA: University of Massachusetts Press, 2003); and *Does Foreign Aid Really Work?* by Roger C. Riddell (Oxford, UK: Oxford University Press, 2008).

5.   In British India, for example, missionaries were allowed to work among Indians only after the 1813 renewal of the Charter of the East India Company by Parliament. The Company had previously argued that missionaries would disrupt India's religious equilibrium. By 1813, the influence of the evangelical "Clapham Sect," led in Parliament by William Wilberforce, was sufficient to amend the Charter in favor of missionaries.

a particular state regards as contrary to the best interests of the whole community" (Wright 2004:289). Thus, in the interests of post-colonial independence, it was logical to restrict or prohibit missionaries; and in the interests of illiberal regimes, it is logical to restrict or prohibit aid workers. The twentieth century is hardly the first period when followers of Jesus have been identified with a foreign power: ancient Persia identified Christians with the Roman Empire in the fourth and fifth centuries, and they were seen as potential enemy agents.

I experienced this dynamic firsthand as an English teacher shortly after the breakup of the former Soviet Union. I had chosen not to use my classroom as a venue for sharing my faith. But one year an American basketball team visited my class with just that intent. I had invited them to the class so that my students could interact with other native speakers of English besides myself. I had not felt it necessary to ask permission from my department head because the team's coordinator had assured me that the players would only tell their personal stories. Yet after their presentation, they passed out evangelistic literature to the students. Had it only been my own students in attendance, the incident might have stopped there. But other students had joined my class that day to meet the Americans, along with my boss and several other local teachers. The following week, I was called to a meeting of my department at which a university official, hitherto unknown to me, was present. He accused me of being a CIA agent sent to subvert his government by creating two religious groups that would fight each other and create a pretext for outside military intervention in the name of peace! To say I was stunned would be an understatement.

My fellow teachers rallied to my defense, as did a higher official to whom I was summoned the next day, and my teaching career continued without interruption. However, on several occasions afterward, my boss told me that if I had given her advance notice, she would have arranged a university-wide event. The university basketball team would have played an exhibition game with the team, and they could then have addressed all those in attendance. Sometimes you need to think big!

Nevertheless, had the hostile official had his way, I would have been on a plane leaving the country the next day. As it was, he was seriously mistaken and everyone else knew it, but his views are not uncommon. The idea that foreigners are dangerous is deeply ingrained in many parts of the world. It exists at some level in almost any country, no matter how liberal that country may be.

An incident at a church I attended, after living in one particular country a number of years, showed me how prevalent this mindset of suspicion can be. I had regularly attended the church for over a year when I was asked to give my testimony in a morning service. The person who introduced me had known me for many months and had always been pleasant and kind to me. So I was shocked when she told everyone she had been certain I was a spy when I had first arrived. She assured the congregation that she now knew she had been mistaken, and that I was harmless. All the same, her comments served as a wake-up call, making me realize how deeply even church members had been conditioned to view foreigners as dangerous.

One might think that fear of foreigners is an overreaction, but in some cases such fear is warranted. Between 2003 and 2005, a number of countries from the former Soviet Union experienced what came to be known as "color revolutions." These were regime changes accomplished largely through nonviolent protests. The protests had been organized with the assistance of pro-democracy organizations funded partially by the United States Department of State. Because of this link, governments throughout the former Soviet Union became suspicious of all nonprofit organizations (known as "non-governmental organizations" or NGOs in many countries), particularly those with foreign funding. A direct link to regime change had been established. Despite the fact that only a few organizations were implicated, all became suspect.

Fear of culture change also has its basis: every society has principles and institutions that hold it together, and culture change can threaten those principles. In the United States, for example, these principles and institutions are defined and enshrined in the Constitution. The rigid and rigorous mechanism for changing the Constitution enables the US to embrace a great deal of diversity and flexibility without any threat to the fundamental fabric of the nation. In many countries, however, less well-defined principles hold the nation together. Whatever formal constitution may exist in such places plays a lesser role in assuring stability. Thus, any person, group, or idea that appears to threaten the fundamental principles in such a place is perceived as a dangerous threat to the nation. Even in America, most conservatives would feel that although the fundamental fabric of the *nation* might not be threatened by great diversity, the fundamental fabric of *society* certainly is. So if Americans, with a strong Constitution and nearly 250-year-old institutions, can feel threatened by diversity, how much more is this true in societies with far less inherent stability?

As for change of an expressly religious nature, it is important to note that fervent religious believers of all kinds can be a direct threat to those in authority for two reasons. First, they acknowledge a higher source of authority which by definition cannot be challenged by human leaders. Second, they do not fear death. When people become fervent believers, they change their priorities and their behavior, and they challenge their leaders to change as well. Over time, such movements tend to become "domesticated" in their culture, losing any prophetic role. This happened to the church in Hitler's Third Reich, for example. But when a religious community is new or newly revived, it will inevitably be seen as a threat by government officials or community elders.

In summary, guests can be a threat to their hosts without any intention of causing harm. Directly or indirectly, intentionally or unintentionally, they may challenge the authority of those who wield power or influence in society. Foreigners may be seen as a threat to the state, to the structures of society; or they may be perceived as such even though they are not. And they are almost certainly a threat to the continuity of the culture. Culture is not static, and cultures are influenced by foreigners even if they do not actually enter a society. But those who do enter will surely leave their traces behind.

WHY GOVERNMENTS INITIATE PROHIBITIONS AND RESTRICTIONS

Before considering the responses of today's governments, let us look at the responses of Jewish leaders to Jesus and his followers. We can assume that much will be the same today, although certain features do not match those of the first century. For one, the concepts we have today about the state, citizens, and expatriates are not at all the same as corresponding concepts of the first century. Second, Jesus and his disciples were not expatriates in Galilee or Judea by any measure; neither was Paul an expatriate in Asia Minor or Greece— these places were both parts of the Roman Empire of which he was a citizen. Nevertheless, the biblical accounts of opposition by leaders are relevant to our situation today, and we will look in some detail at the relevant texts.

In Jesus' case, the religious leaders of the time (who were also community leaders more broadly) opposed him and his disciples almost without exception. As the Roman governor Pilate aptly observed, this opposition was rooted in envy, or as the new NIV translation puts it, self-interest (Matt 27:18; Mark 15:10). Pilate interpreted the conflict between Jesus and the Jewish leaders as a competition for power and influence.

Acts 5:17 speaks of "jealousy" (NIV) that led Jerusalem's religious leaders to oppose Peter and John when they spoke and taught about Jesus. The word used is not the same as the "envy" in Matthew 27 and Mark 15. Rather, it is the Greek root (via different derivations) of the English words "zeal" and "jealousy." One of these words is positive and the other negative, but what they have in common is intense feeling. The *cause* of the intense feeling must be determined from context. In Acts 5:17, the context suggests that the opposition here might have involved doctrinal issues as well as personal rivalry: the dominant religious leaders of the time were Sadducees, who did not believe in the life after death proclaimed by Peter and John (Acts 4:1,2). The doctrinal reason for their jealousy was a concern for truth that opposes anything considered heretical. Yet such "jealousy for truth" rarely exists without an accompanying personal envy. By the same token, personal envy is often mixed with true concern for the well-being of one's community.

Further examples of jealousy with both community and personal roots can be found later in Acts, in the accounts of opposition to Paul from Jewish community leaders in Asia Minor and in Greece (Acts 13:45 and 17:5). In Acts 13:45, jealousy appears to be more personal: it is aroused when the leaders "saw the crowds." But in Acts 17:5, the fact that some "were jealous" is mentioned just after discussion of others who were persuaded by Paul, suggesting a doctrinal basis for the jealousy again. The Greek words in both passages have the same root as in Acts 5:17—"intense feeling." New Testament scholar Richard Longenecker notes that in Thessalonica (Acts 17), the intense feeling may have had something to do with the expulsion of Jews from Rome due to conflicts there between followers of Jesus and other Jews. The Thessalonian Jews may have feared "that such a situation might be duplicated at Thessalonica" (1981:469).

In his discussion of Acts 13, Longenecker raises a deeper source of opposition: "from Luke's perspective opposition to the gospel is directed not so much against the messengers as against the content of the message—Jesus himself" (1981:429). As Paul told King Agrippa, "I too was convinced that I ought to do all that was possible to oppose the name of Jesus of Nazareth" (Acts 26:9). Paul makes clear that his opposition was directed at Jesus himself, and Jesus says the same thing in Acts 9: "Why do you persecute me?" and "I am Jesus, whom you are persecuting" (vv. 4,5).

Such opposition to the name of Jesus also exists today. However—and this point cannot be emphasized too strongly—how can we be sure that a particular act of opposition to our presence is, at heart, opposition to Jesus himself and not merely to us? Instead of simply assuming such opposition is directed against Jesus, we should also look for ordinary human causes. Doing so can help us see those who oppose us as fellow humans in need of the Savior. If they are our enemies, we need to love them as Jesus commanded us to do. On the other hand, if we see people as enemies of Jesus, we may somehow conclude that since these are not *our* enemies but Jesus' enemies, we are not required to love them. This is another reason we should search for human reasons for their opposition.

In the Epistle to the Ephesians, Paul raises yet another source of opposition to followers of Christ, in which human actors appear merely as pawns of spiritual forces: "our struggle is not against flesh and blood" (6:12). In response, we are called to "put on the full armor of God" (v. 13)—truth, righteousness, the gospel of peace, faith, salvation, and the word of God—and at all times, to pray. These are crucial preparations for service to Jesus. Nevertheless, not every difficulty can be reduced to spiritual attack. Doing so oversimplifies matters and overlooks the non-supernatural causes of opposition. Moreover, when we write home about "spiritual attack," it makes us appear more righteous than we are, and better servants of Jesus than we are. It is therefore important to understand as many of the reasons behind opposition as possible, rather than reducing it to any single cause. Perhaps because of the tendency to reduce difficulty to spiritual attack, and opposition to enmity toward Christ, missionary guests rarely consider that the changes they bring might not all be positive.

Let us look at the human reasons for opposition. For a start, even in an open democracy, those in power tend to show annoyance with anyone who objects to their program, and to belittle their political opponents. In an authoritarian context, authorities are openly hostile to all who oppose them. Since expatriate workers, whether they are religious or secular, almost always have their own program regardless of the authorities, they will often be a source of annoyance—and not just to Almorian authorities. Christy Wilson (1981), who served many years in Central Asia, reminds us that opposition to sent ones comes as often from the officials of liberal democracies as it does from officials of restrictive countries.

Another reason for opposition may simply be that officials hope for financial gain through bribes that might be offered to overcome obstacles in the way of visas or other permissions. Applications for visas or work permits are an obvious place where a "tip" can grease the bureaucratic machinery. If one is from a country where corruption is low, or only exists at the highest levels of power, the thought of giving a bribe does not even cross one's mind; one simply gets annoyed at the red tape and how long it takes to get things done. But if one is from a more corrupt country, the idea that someone would *not* offer a bribe may be the one that does not cross the mind. And Almorian officials might interpret such a refusal as simply an attempt to push the price down, or as evidence of either lack of funds or mere stupidity. I am not suggesting that giving a bribe is the right response in such an instance; I am merely noting that the hope of receiving a bribe is sometimes the true cause of obstacles encountered from local officials.

A context in which a bribe may be the goal is when one is stopped on the street by police. Often, this procedure is a routine check of documents (so make sure that yours are in order, and carry photocopies for routine use), but it can also lead to more. Ralph, a young intercultural worker in the capital city of Almoria, had not been there long before he was pulled to one side in front of the city's main department store. A plainclothes official directed him into a side office of the store, clearly marked "POLICE." Ralph complied, and the officer proceeded to search Ralph's backpack for drugs. Ralph later realized how naïve he had been—and how fortunate he was to have been released immediately. Others told stories of drugs being planted on them in similar situations, and warned strongly against going into any office with police, suggesting rather that one insist everything be done in public view. Even after many years in Almoria, Ralph's instinctive reaction when accosted by a plainclothes officer was to run: it feels like you are being assaulted. But of course, running only makes an officer angry and all the more suspicious.

Before moving on to consider types of restrictions, let us remember that by far the most common government response to expatriates is to ignore them. This response even applies when the secret police are aware that an expatriate is doing something that would be opposed by some segments of society. In cities with many expatriates, secret police may not be aware of everything simply because they lack personnel to monitor every expatriate. But it is still good to assume that they know everything they want to know and that all forms of communication are monitored. Nevertheless, the most common government response is inaction, especially if the expatriates in question (or their national colleagues and friends, for that matter) are keeping a low profile and not drawing the attention of those in society who would oppose their presence.

At some point, even when individual expatriates have been keeping a low profile, their overall impact may begin to be felt, and the authorities may initiate action in response. The first step in many places comes in the form of indirect hints, particularly in cultures that value politeness, hospitality, or indirect communication. Central Asian hospitality, for example, follows the maxim, *"Kel degen bar, ket degen jok,"* which indicates that you can invite guests, but there's no asking them to leave. This cultural requirement can be very strong, and leads to indirect communication. In the case of governments, an increase in the visa fee or in the complexity of the visa application process may well be intended as a hint that the overall number of foreigners is more than desired. Sometimes delays or complications in visa applications are intended as such hints. But if local colleagues or friends have extended a warm and clear invitation, it is usually appropriate to ignore indirect communications by officials and press on with attempts to obtain permission to stay. The "hints" may also be ways of soliciting bribes, and not veiled messages telling the guests to leave. Of course, if hosts are asking their guests for bribes, they are certainly not conveying a welcoming message!

At some point, especially if the expatriate has done something to draw particular attention, or if a specific "raid" was initiated by authorities, the indirect communication comes to an end. In most cases, expulsion will be the worst consequence, although this is not a hard and fast rule. British agents in Bukhara in the nineteenth century were imprisoned and sometimes executed, and workers have been murdered more recently in various parts of the world. The British in Bukhara were assumed to be spying; workers today may face the same assumption, or may be blamed for other "crimes."

Even in cases of expulsion, imprisonment, or execution, opposition arises just as often for political reasons as for spiritual ones. In 2006, for example, numerous expatriate organizations were expelled from Uzbekistan. Some were completely secular, some less so. The reason for their expulsion had little to do with their activities and much more to do with the critical response Uzbekistan had received from the United States and the European Union after Uzbek authorities massacred hundreds of citizens who opposed the government in the city of Andijan. A few organizations were allowed to remain, although some of them were ultimately expelled in succeeding years.

Three observations about restrictive and repressive governments are important to note. First, restrictions and repression vary with time, place, and person. A "no" today may be a "yes" in a year's time, and activities that go unhindered today may be repressed next month. Also, some places in a given country are more restrictive or repressive than others. Some embassies or entry points are more generous with visas than others. Interpretation and enforcement will differ from official to official, even in the same location during the same time period. Taking advantage of these variations requires constant vigilance because they can work both ways. After one has enjoyed a more relaxed atmosphere for a time, one may not be alert to a sudden change for the worse. One has to be attentive all the time. And then, as a Korean friend once said to me, "When the wind blows, hide behind a rock."

The second observation concerns places that truly are extremely restrictive. Brother Andrew, author of *God's Smuggler* and founder of Open Doors, has pointed out that some situations are so repressive that followers of Jesus may not be able to do more than just *be* there—a ministry of "presence" (Andrew 1998:42). That presence has value in itself. Even there, though, the reality on the ground will not always be as restrictive as the spoken rhetoric. There are countries where public meetings of Jesus' followers are strictly illegal and yet they happen. The government rhetoric seeks to satisfy the most conservative members of society, but some officials may be less conservative. They may be content to give lip service to written restrictions as long as "violations" occur quietly and unobtrusively.

My final observation concerns the way that sent ones report news about restrictive situations. Exaggerations are not uncommon. Sometimes this happens when a number of countries are lumped together in a report, and less restrictive countries are made to seem no different from the most restrictive. At other times, an event may be over-dramatized or made to seem like it is commonplace when in fact it is not. Such statements can make one's ministry seem more exciting or more worthwhile, and they may even be made quite unintentionally, but they distort the perspective of their readers. This is not to say that extreme restrictions never exist, but merely to point out that even people of integrity exaggerate at times.

The reader may object that I am being too harsh on sent ones. After all, most are dedicated servants, faithfully assisting the people to whom they were called and submitting to those in authority. They try to be culturally sensitive and seek to avoid negative outcomes from their presence. Is it not better for a country to interact with expatriates of goodwill, such as sent ones, than with those seeking to take advantage of their hosts? Is it not better to have personal contact with representatives of other cultures than to merely be bombarded by foreign media? The authorities have nothing to be concerned about from sent ones, do they? True. But if the authorities do not know this, it doesn't help us that it is true. Also, because we know we are people of goodwill, we are all the more inclined to attribute opposition or difficulty to spiritual causes. Yet more often than not the causes of difficulty are quite mundane.

Having thought about all these things, how should expatriate followers of Jesus respond to Almorian authorities?

RESPONDING TO AUTHORITIES IN THE SPIRIT OF CHRIST

Because government opposition to expatriate workers often has mundane causes, we should pay attention to the reasons behind restrictions, spiritual or otherwise, and make necessary adjustments to our approach. Even so, these adjustments cannot guarantee a smooth relationship with authorities.

Sometimes you may be called in for questioning by local police officials wondering who you are and what you are doing. Some suggest that in restrictive countries with few expatriates it is good to visit the local authorities *before* being summoned—as soon as possible after your arrival, in fact. You can make your presence known, ask how you can practice your faith without trouble, and even find out under what conditions it would be acceptable to talk about your faith. This keeps the initiative on your side, and may prevent an unpleasant visit from the authorities later. Most of all, it helps them to place you and to understand you. They are wondering about you already, so is it not best to give them your own account of yourself right away? If they know you are not benefiting financially by being in their country, then they will be particularly curious as to why you are there.

Some might object that presenting yourself to the relevant authorities puts you on their radar unnecessarily. Such an attitude assumes that you have something to fear from the authorities. Perhaps you are concerned that they would expel you if they knew you were a follower of Jesus who is not averse to sharing Jesus with others. Assuming for now that this is a legitimate concern, a further question needs to be asked: Would you remain unknown to the authorities if you did not present yourself? The answer may depend on how many expatriates live in your city. Even if you would be known to them without presenting yourself, would going to them yourself encourage them to pay a return visit to you? They might even think you have money to give them.

I myself prefer a low profile—it is more in keeping with my personality. Nevertheless, I recognize the value of going to the official. Doing so tells him I am not cowering in a corner. It says I am showing him respect and honor, while at the same time I am not afraid of his power. I have a question to ask him (such as "How can I practice and share my faith in your country?"), so my visit has a purpose. I would probably first go to whatever person was responsible for me at my work and perhaps ask that person to accompany me to see the police officer responsible for my area of residence. I might even go higher than that, to someone in the secret police. If the person at my work discouraged me from going to other officials, I would seek to understand why and would probably follow their advice. But at the same time I would stress to them that my true and complete purpose was transparent and therefore I had nothing to fear from any official.

When answering the authorities' questions, it is important to discern what they are looking for. They are tasked with protecting their people from danger, so they have a right to investigate and determine whether or not you present a threat. The deep suspicion of foreigners' motives in many countries has a painful history behind it: there have been incidents in the past that justify suspicion. My experience of the woman in my church thinking I was a spy, and the accusation from the university official following the visit of the American basketball team, are just two examples of this suspicion.

In their defense, how are Almorians to know that you mean well and have no ulterior purpose?

George, an expatriate worker in a former Soviet country, was called in by the secret police soon after his arrival. When asked why he was there, he answered that God had called him there. The official immediately relaxed when he heard this; he believed it to be a true answer indicating that George was not a spy, which was his primary concern. After that visit, during more than five years in that country, George had no trouble with officials, although other sent ones were repeatedly hassled.

However, one story does not prove a point; the opposite outcome may have occurred just as many times. The deeper question concerns our attitude toward officials. Do we see them primarily as a threat, or primarily as people in need of a Savior? Certainly everyone is in need of the Savior. As to seeing officials as a threat, many ordinary Almorians see them that way, and avoid them for that reason. But this view of officials has nothing to do with their being a particular threat to those who follow Jesus. Although the Bible teaches that followers of Jesus should expect persecution (Mark 13:13; 2 Tim 3:12), this does not mean we should interpret every occasion of difficulty or official harassment as persecution for Jesus' sake. Nor should we look at every Almorian official as a probable persecutor. There have been instances where sent ones had an ongoing relationship with their local representative of the secret police. Such stories may not prove any general principle, but they do suggest that workers' fears of secret police are overblown.

Regardless of our view of officials—or their view of us—we are called to pray for them: "that we may live peaceful and quiet lives in all godliness and holiness" (1 Tim 2:1–2). Such a prayer can take a number of forms. We can pray quietly among ourselves and await with faith what God will do. We can also expect that on occasion, God will give opportunities to pray directly for officials or to bless them in other ways. These opportunities have a way of turning up when we least expect them and are preoccupied with our own difficulties. One worker, Albert, had such an opportunity *after* he had been told to leave Almoria and never return. On his way out at the airport, Albert asked the police officer escorting him if he could pray for the officer's sick relative before he left. He did not have specific knowledge of a sick relative but assumed that someone among the man's relatives must be ill. In this particular case, the request to pray led to an extension of Albert's time in the country. My father relates a similar story about a dentist named Fred who had been given two days to leave his country of service. That very day, however, he encountered an official in the foreign ministry who had a terrible tooth abscess. Fred treated the man, and was then granted an additional two years in the country. These things do happen!

We can also pray for our own response to difficulties and for God's ongoing work, as the Jerusalem believers did after Peter and John faced opposition from the religious leaders (Acts 4:29,30). Peter and John had just been released after being warned not to speak or teach any more in Jesus' name. They joined the other believers and prayed that they would continue to speak boldly and that God would continue to heal and to do wonders through the name of Jesus. This prayer did not guarantee them protection from future harm, but it did help them to speak boldly—especially when "the place where they were meeting was shaken" after they had prayed (Acts 4:31). In the case of expatriate workers, praying may not guarantee against deportation, but it will certainly accomplish something, as the prayer of faith always does.

The prayers in Acts 4 and 1 Timothy 2 focus on our own lives and ministry, even though they arise in response to officials' power over believers. In other places in the New Testament, however, we are called to go deeper than praying about our own situations. Romans 12:14 sums it up in this manner: "Bless those who persecute you. Bless and do not curse." Matthew 5:44 asks us to pray for those who persecute us, and Luke 6:28 for those who mistreat us. The root of the matter is found in Matthew 5:44 and Luke 6:27 and 6:35: "Love your enemies." If we face direct opposition, for whatever reason, we still have the opportunity to pray for those who oppose us. Jesus calls us to love and to pray and to bless without any thought for what may come in return (Matt 5:46,47; Luke 6:32–35).

Praying for and loving those in authority does not necessarily imply that we should obey them. The Bible instructs us to honor those in authority (Rom 13:7; 1 Pet 2:17), and not to fear them unless we have done something wrong. But this does not mean that Romans 13:1–10 and 1 Peter 2:12–17 support complete submission to any government just because Romans 13:1 says that the authorities that exist have been established by God. The passage in Acts that we have considered—Acts 4:18–31, and also its continuation in 5:12–42—shows Peter and John refusing to obey the command of the Jewish authorities who insisted that they refrain from speaking about Jesus. Peter and John based their refusal on a simple principle: "We must obey God rather than human beings" (Acts 5:29). The apparent contradiction between Acts and Romans/1 Peter can be resolved if we remember that God's sovereignty over human rulers (*and* over the people ruled) takes precedence over the rulers' sovereignty. According to New Testament scholar Everett Harrison, Paul probably uses the word "submit" in Romans 13:1 rather than "the stronger word 'obey'" because "the believer may find it impossible to comply with every demand of the government. A circumstance may arise in which he must choose between obeying God and obeying men (Act 5:29)" (1976:136–37).

What are some implications of this conclusion? What does it mean in practice to obey God rather than men? It does not mean we are free to disobey or disregard every regulation that does not suit us or which appears to obstruct our goals. Disobeying human authorities is justified only when obeying God clearly requires disobeying the authorities. But "clearly requires" can be interpreted differently by different people; some cases are clear cut, others are more complex. Simply put, there is a tension between the call to obey those in authority and the call to obey God. Let us consider some of the complexities as they pertain to service in Almoria.

We know that obeying God takes precedence over obeying a government's laws or an official's demands. Does this mean that fulfilling our calling—which we consider to be obeying God—also takes precedence? If we say yes, then we are making the faulty assumption that our ability to know our calling is both perfect and complete. Although we may have a correct understanding of the *what* of our calling, we may be in error about the *how*, the *when*, and the *where* of it. So it is not right to assume automatically that everything we include in our sense of calling is an essential part of obeying God. We so easily confuse our own plans and desires for a particular ministry, or for a presence in a particular place, with God's desires. Followers of Jesus, especially those who are expatriates in a foreign country, should humbly seek understanding of what God is doing in a particular place and time before making assumptions about their role in it.

Conversely, we must not fall into the opposite trap of using these considerations as an excuse for doing nothing. For example, if Peter had done an in-depth analysis of the concerns and needs of the religious leaders before he healed the lame beggar in Acts 3, he probably would have left the beggar sitting by the temple gate. He would have missed the opportunity not only to bless the beggar, but to also explain to the worshipers at the temple what he had done. Note also that Peter and John did not set out that afternoon with the intention of performing miracles. They were simply "going up to the temple at the time of prayer" (Acts 3:1), and Peter responded to the beggar's request for money by healing him in Jesus' name. Everything else flowed on from that—including the trouble with the authorities. In the same way, we need to take the opportunities that God gives us as we go about our daily routine.

But unplanned opportunities such as Peter's healing of the lame man are not the focus of this discussion about the various reasons for opposition. Rather, the focus is on our longer-term vocational and strategic choices. When we make these choices, we need to take seriously the human reasons behind restrictions or hostility from authorities. We need to think carefully about our overall attitude toward authorities when it comes to their restrictions or their administrative requirements.

How then should followers of Jesus respond if a government requires that they register as religious workers, clearly disclosing any religious intent? When we look at Jesus and Paul we see that their disclosure was in their deeds, not in any statement of registration. Jesus disclosed himself and his purposes in differing degrees. Often, he told those he had healed not to tell others about what had happened to them. To his disciples, however, he revealed more, and to Peter, James, and John—the closest of his disciples—he revealed the most. But neither Jesus nor Paul were required to register as religious workers, nor did they belong to any formally constituted international organization.

Indeed, our context is far from Jesus and Paul's. In considering whether or not to register, or how to declare ourselves, we must take many factors into account. Sometimes we may not fit any of the government's categories or we may disagree with the government's definitions. Others have found that registration gives them more freedom, even if it means they are being watched more closely. A crucial factor to consider is the simple matter of who we are: there must be consistency between what we say about ourselves and what we do.

A final implication of obeying God rather than human authorities is that we will have to face the consequences when we make this choice. As Harrison puts it, Romans 13:1 teaches that when we choose to obey God rather than men, we still submit to the consequences (1976:137). Jesus taught us to expect persecution as a consequence (Luke 21:12–17; John 15:20–21). The Apostles were flogged (Acts 5:40) and ultimately, according to church tradition, all but one were executed. In our world, citizens of powerful countries are less likely to face that kind of consequence, but we must still be prepared.

Other biblical examples provide insight into what it means to obey God rather than human authorities. Throughout Scripture we find a consistent emphasis on obeying God over human rulers. Sometimes that involves disobeying edicts, such as the Hebrew midwives disobeying Pharaoh's decree to kill Hebrew boys (Ex 1:15–21), or Daniel (and Shadrach, Meshach, and Abednego) disobeying the royal edict against bowing down or praying to others besides the king (Dan 3 and 6). At other times it involved speaking out against rulers, such as Moses challenging Pharaoh in Exodus, Nathan confronting David in 2 Samuel 12, and Elijah's challenge to Ahab and Jezebel in 1 Kings 17–19. Jeremiah and other prophets spoke out repeatedly against the wrongs of the kings of Judah, and Esther broke the ban against approaching the king without being summoned in order to save her people (Esth 4:16). We find God himself judging both priest (Eli) and king (Saul) and finding them wanting, in 1 Samuel 3:11–14 and 15:10–29. And Jesus takes a strong stand against the religious leaders of his day. We have already seen the apostles in Acts.

All of these biblical characters serve as examples for us. Christopher J. H. Wright, in his book *Old Testament Ethics for the People of God*, particularly advocates Daniel as a model for us in dealing with governments:

> The subtlety and mature balance of Daniel's stance is remarkable. On the one hand, knowing that it was God himself who had given Nebuchadnezzar all authority and dominion, he nevertheless did not feel bound to obey Nebuchadnezzar in every particular. . . . *Daniel's doctrine of the divine appointment of human authority did not make him a passive pawn, giving uncritical obedience to the particular authority under which he lived.* But, on the other hand, . . . *Daniel's doctrine of the satanic influence on human powers did not make him withdraw as an escapist from political involvement.* (2004:247, italics in original)

Daniel shows us that we are neither to blindly accept a regime's rules nor to blindly assume that every statute stands opposed to God's justice and that any form of cooperation with the regime is evil. Perhaps some regimes are so completely evil that nothing short of direct and complete opposition is an acceptable position for the people of God. But I cannot think of any such regime in today's world, even though some are clearly more evil than others. Followers of Jesus should avoid blind responses to any government, no matter where they live.

A number of the biblical examples we have just considered involved speaking out when rulers were wrong. To what extent is this part of a biblical response to Almorian authorities and their restrictions on expatriate followers of Jesus? Although this question gets into matters well beyond the scope of this book—the issue of how believers should relate to wrongdoing by authorities is a huge topic—a few questions are worth raising.

First of all, if one feels obliged to speak out, what is that sense of obligation based on? Is it simply an impression that obedience to God requires it? Is it for conscience? Is it to take a stand, or to make a difference? In the cases of Moses and Esther, it was to make a difference. In both of those cases, though, it was ultimately not Moses or Esther who made the difference but *God* who moved the heart of the ruler through the agency of Moses and Esther. Or the motivation for speaking out may be to help the downtrodden, in keeping with the character of God, who "defends the cause of the fatherless and the widow, and loves the foreigner" (Deut 10:18), and to heed the call of Psalm 82:3-4,

> Defend the weak and the fatherless;
> uphold the cause of the poor and the oppressed.
> Rescue the weak and the needy;
> deliver them from the hand of the wicked.

Whatever the reason may be, if one concludes that speaking out is needed, another question is *how* to do so. Should a believer speak out as an individual, or only in agreement with the full body of believers? Such agreement may be hard to reach. Additionally, should one speak out publicly, to expose the wrongdoing, or go privately to the official concerned? Should one fight on until full justice is achieved, or be satisfied with some level of change?

One young expatriate worker in Almoria objected when she was asked by a university official to include a relative of the university president in a special English class, even though the relative had fared poorly in the entrance exam. The official's response was a surprising one: "You should see how many people approached me and tried to get their kids into your class!" he said. "I turned them all away. But this one you need to accept."

The young teacher struggled with this advice from the official, but accepted her seasoned intercultural team leader's suggestion that she admit the president's relative into the class. As it turned out, doing so opened up a good relationship with the official concerned, and many opportunities for deep conversations ensued. Perhaps her initial revulsion at apparent nepotism was too strong a reaction. Still, she sometimes wondered if she had done the right thing.

Remember that an expatriate guest may simply be expelled for speaking out against authorities, especially if it is done publicly. Whole organizations have been expelled because of the actions of one of their members. Is it not better to stay and have *some* influence rather than to be kicked out altogether? And is it not appropriate for a guest to keep quiet and let national believers stand up for righteousness in their country? This argument has some legitimacy, but it is surely an oversimplification. It cannot be right to stand back out of harm's way ourselves but push our national brothers and sisters into confrontation with their country's leaders. Yet if we are simply ejected from the country, what help is that to the nationals we leave behind? The issue is indeed not simple.[6]

---

6. See *Good News About Injustice* (IVP, 1999), by Gary Haugen of International Justice Mission, for a helpful discussion of the varying roles of nationals and expatriates in combating injustice.

In deciding whether or not to speak out, or in choosing an appropriate response to government opposition or restrictions, all followers of Jesus should heed his words and be "as shrewd as snakes and as innocent as doves" (Matt 10:16). Rick Love makes the following comments on that verse which are worth quoting in full:

> Why are snakes described as shrewd or wise? Because they fit in with their environment with their camouflage skin, they don't draw attention to themselves. They get the job done but remain low-profile. If you put a snake on a lawn it will seek a place to hide in nearby bushes or rocks.
>
> But we are not just called to be snake-like "undercover agents." Jesus says we must also be as innocent as doves. The Greek term for innocence refers to character marked by integrity, innocence of evil and purity.
>
> What a powerful yet difficult balance to maintain. In the context of persecution and danger (Remember the wolves!), we should be low profile, yet remain guileless—be wary but wear no masks. Snake-like behavior alone can become devious. Dove-like behavior alone can become gullible. Together these images forge a striking apostolic identity that will maximize our fruitfulness. (www.ricklove.net)

Robert Morris, who served for many years in South Asia and in organizational leadership, has also commented on Matthew 10:16 in an article written to urge shrewdness. But he begins with this qualifier: "We must never use our shrewdness in a hypocritical or deceptive way, nor be naïve or stupid" (1998:5). Again, this is a difficult balance to maintain. Only Jesus has done it perfectly, and only Jesus can enable us to emulate his example to any degree at all.

In seeking to understand Matthew 10:16, we need to under-stand its context: the chapter depicts the sending out of the Twelve to proclaim the kingdom of heaven, to cast out demons, and to minister healing among "the lost sheep of Israel" (vv. 6–8). The sending of the Twelve—Israelites sent to other Israelites—is *not* an example of intercultural outreach. Nevertheless, being "as shrewd as snakes and as innocent as doves" certainly applies as much to intercultural outreach as to the sending of the Twelve.

The next point to note is that Jesus gives the Twelve authority over demons and disease but not over other people, as is clearly seen when one looks at the full text. The disciples are dependent on generous hosts (vv. 9–13) and subject to cruel rulers (vv. 16–23), much as Jesus himself was (vv. 24,25). Jesus did give them authority for the day of judgment (vv. 14,15) but not for this life. In this life, Jesus' followers must be ready to lose everything (vv. 34–39) for publicly acknowledging their Lord (vv. 32,33). Being shrewd yet innocent clearly does not mean always getting out of difficulties.

Further, the sent ones are called to "speak in the daylight" and "proclaim from the roofs" what Jesus told them "in the dark" or what was "whispered in [their] ear" (v. 27). Being shrewd yet innocent, in their case, clearly does not mean keeping these things hidden in order to avoid difficulties. And although they may flee (v. 23), they must not be afraid (vv. 26, 28), even though they are sent out as "sheep among wolves" (v. 16). This, then, is the context in which they should be as shrewd as snakes and as innocent as doves: bold proclamation and healing, without fear and without secrets.

We can also learn from examples in today's world of what it means to obey God rather than people. One group of expatriates, faced with Almorian laws that increasingly restricted religious freedom, sought to distinguish between those activities God requires of all believers and those which are only required from people with a specific calling. They concluded that gathering for prayer and worship and fellowship, sharing one's faith with others, and in particular instructing one's children in the word of God, were clearly expected of God from all believers, foreign or national. The time and place and way of doing these things could vary from person to person and from place to place. The activities the group felt believers were not obligated to do unless they had a specific calling from God included preaching in a church, door-to-door witnessing, and widespread literature distribution. Preaching and up-front leadership, they felt, are best done by nationals anyway. Interestingly, speaking out against injustice did not appear in either the obligatory or the optional category. This goes to show that any such list reflects the priorities of those who make it.

A second example comes from one individual, Frank, working in a restrictive country. Over the course of time, Frank had seen a number of people come to follow Jesus. He met with them regularly to help them grow closer to Jesus. One day, an agent of the secret police informed Frank that he must no longer associate with those people. "They are bad people," he was told. Frank continued to associate with them. Then he got a second warning. This time, Frank was told that continued association with them would mean he would have to leave the country; the secret police officials realized they would need to be explicit with Frank to help him stay within the accepted bounds. Frank knew they were trying to "help" him, and he had cultivated a respectful relationship with them. What should he do?

As he considered the matter, Frank came to the firm conviction that he must continue meeting with those whom he was discipling. Not to do so, even if he were to explain the reason to them, would set the wrong example for them. The next time he met his friends, he told them he most likely would not see them again, and encouraged them to continue meeting together to study the Scriptures and pray together. He turned out to be right. Within the month, he was deported.

In conclusion, should we obey restrictive governments or ignore their decrees? There is no one-size-fits-all answer to that question. We should, however, be careful before following the argument that "the government is opposing God so I don't need to obey the government." All too often, we justify disobeying restrictive governments by defining any restriction of our freedom as religious persecution. Instead, whenever it is possible without disobeying God, we should obey the authorities—even if we disagree with their laws.

Ultimately, one must follow one's own conscience to navigate the tension between obeying God and obeying human authorities. But we mustn't forget that even the conscience is influenced by culture and by personality. One way to reduce this influence is to err in the opposite direction of our natural inclinations. In other words, if our inclination is always to comply with authority, perhaps we should be more prepared to speak out or even to disobey; if our inclination is to rebel, we should err in the direction of compliance. Whatever we choose, let us refrain from judging those who choose differently, even if a brother or sister's action (or inaction) hurts or harms us.

STEPS FOR ACTION, REFLECTION AND GROUP DISCUSSION

1. In what ways do you put projects before people? When is it legitimate to do so? Or is it never okay? Take steps to make any needed changes in your priorities.
2. Think of ways in which foreign aid may in fact be an expression of domination, not of service. See http://honorshame.com/how-to-give-aid-without-shaming/
3. Think about the role of a guest. In what ways might you be in danger of taking the host's position because you control too much of the agenda? How can you know when it is time for you, the guest, to leave—or to become a permanent resident or citizen? How can you know when to keep quiet and when to speak?

4. What kind of problems can arise when you have more money than your hosts? In this chapter we looked at issues of control related to money; in Chapter 4 and 5 we will discuss differences in living standards.

5. Examine your own attitudes: to what extent do you share the common misperception that wealth, technology, or democracy make one society better or more civilized than another? What concrete steps can you take to adopt a more humble attitude? If there is a group you might be tempted to look down on, are there people from that group or a similar group whom you could get to know? Find out what they value about their culture and community; this may take more digging than a simple "What do you like?" question. Even if you do not come to value it yourself, your understanding of their perspective will broaden your own.

6. How would your response change if you discovered that the opposition you face from officials was against you, not against Jesus?

7. Think of your calling. Has God shown you how, when, and where you are to serve, as well as what you are to do there? What steps are appropriate to take before all the pieces are in place, and what steps should wait?

CHAPTER TWO

SECRECY AND PRIVACY, HONESTY AND INTEGRITY

We must be men and women of integrity, through and through.

Secrecy in the service of intercultural outreach seems a questionable strategy. Yet withholding information about oneself is a common practice among sent ones in the process of obtaining a visa or work permit for Almoria. If workers are bothered by the practice, they may justify it by the importance of the work. But that justification suffers from the same problems as any ends-based argument: it ignores the crucial question of means. When the appropriateness of withholding information is discussed as a means, there is considerable disagreement among followers of Jesus: is withholding information tantamount to lying, or is it simply necessary shrewdness? Or is it purely a matter of cultural relativity—normal in one culture but frowned on in another?

This chapter looks at both the ethical problems of a hidden identity as a means, as well as at potential unintended effects of a hidden-identity approach. Justifications of the hidden-identity approach based on one or two Bible passages are discussed but not accepted, because the whole counsel of Scripture is needed in evaluating hidden identity, not merely a few isolated passages.

ATTEMPTS AT JUSTIFYING HIDDEN IDENTITY AND THE WITHHOLDING OF INFORMATION

Are there legitimate reasons for not "telling our enemy what he has no right or business to know" (Andrew 1985:115)? Concealing from an enemy what he has no right to know in the first place could be a powerful defense of the hidden-identity approach, but this justification poses two problems. First, although there may be valid reasons to view Almorian authorities as enemies, this is not a helpful way to look at them; they too are people to be loved in Jesus' name. Second, a host has a right to know a guest's business, and this means Almorian authorities have the right to know what expatriate guests are planning to do in Almoria.

Some have attempted to defend the hidden-identity approach by using Bible texts that specifically deal with hiding information— or one's true purpose—from hostile authorities. Some of these passages have already been mentioned in our general discussion of obeying God, not human authorities. For example, the Hebrew midwives in Egypt refused to carry out Pharaoh's order to kill male babies and then told Pharaoh that Hebrew women "give birth before the midwives arrive" (Ex 1:15–21). As is often the case in the Bible, no direct comment is made about the truth or falsehood of their statement to the king, but they are praised for their courage and loyalty to God's people. Another story is that of Rahab hiding the Israelite spies in Joshua 2, where she tells her king's men that the spies had been there but had left (v. 5). In Hebrews 11:31, Rahab is commended for welcoming the spies. Again, no direct comment is made about her having deceived the king. As Old Testament scholar John Goldingay puts it, the writers of these passages "drive us to do our own reflection on their story" (2003:38).

In the context of Jesus' command to love our enemies—hostile authorities included—reflection on these passages suggests that they do not in fact justify a hidden-identity approach. What they *do* is illustrate the complexity of conflicting ethical demands— such as a sense that the importance of one's mission outweighs the importance of openness. In other words, they help us understand the impetus behind the hidden-identity approach and help us not to condemn those who follow it.

The story of the prophet Samuel's anointing of David, which was mentioned in the Introduction, is sometimes used to support the hidden-identity approach, although I will argue that the passage does not in fact serve that purpose. In 1 Samuel 16:1, God tells Samuel to anoint a son of Jesse to be the future king of Israel. Samuel objects that the current king, Saul, will kill him, and in reply, God tells Samuel to go and make a sacrifice with Jesse at Bethlehem (vv. 2,3). Preempting further objections from Samuel, God reassures him by saying "I will show you what to do" (v. 3). Samuel does make a sacrifice, and he also anoints David. He suffers no retribution from Saul; in fact, God brings retribution on Saul by taking his Spirit from him (v. 14). Samuel's mission was entirely successful, and he did not have to tell any untruths in the process. He said he was going to make a sacrifice, and he did so.

Yet Samuel's primary purpose was not his stated purpose. Was God's direction, then, a form of deception? As in the story of Rahab, the text makes no comment. Commentators throughout history have disagreed about whether the sacrifice was a pretext for the anointing or whether it had its own separate purpose in God's command to Samuel. All agree that God would never command someone to deceive another person; however, most commentators affirm that telling only part of the truth is acceptable if one's hearer can believe what is true from what has been said. In other words, if the hearer comes away believing something distinctly false, then deception has occurred; otherwise, it has not.

Christian workers using the hidden-identity approach feel that they are doing the same thing as Samuel did: telling part of the truth without practicing deception. The problem with this argument is that Samuel was engaged in a one-time symbolic act when he anointed David. Sent ones following the hidden-identity approach, on the other hand, are hiding their identity on a daily basis over many years. Not only that, but Samuel's anointing of David was a hidden agenda, not a hidden identity. As I pointed out in the Introduction, Samuel's *identity* was never in question: he was the prophet of God.

A better known passage that is used to support a hidden-identity approach is found in John 7. Here Jesus was "purposely staying away from Judea because the Jews there [read "local community leaders"] were waiting to take his life" (v. 1). But the Feast of Tabernacles (v. 2) was a time when people from all over Israel went up to Jerusalem, which was in the heart of Judea. So Jesus' brothers, who we read "did not believe in him" (v. 5), taunt him to go and be public. He responds, "The right time for me is not yet here" (v. 6) and says that he is "not yet going up to this Feast" (v. 8). Some early manuscripts do not have "yet;" critics have suggested that it was added to the later manuscripts to preserve Jesus' integrity since he then *did* go (v. 10). The *Expositor's Bible Commentary* says, "The secret departure for Jerusalem was not an act of deception. It was an attempt to avoid unwelcome publicity" (Tenney 1990:82). Whatever one makes of the textual variation, the author surely was not attempting to portray Jesus as less than truthful. Going to Jerusalem "in secret" (v. 10) is not a case of deception. So what *is* going on in this passage?

To answer that question we need to know why Jesus went secretly. The answer is given in the text: "because for me the right time has not yet come" (John 7:8). But the right time for *what*? For going up to the Feast or for going to Jerusalem at all, or for declaring himself publicly and facing the death that he knew must come? Perhaps all of the above. John 7:8 is not the only passage in the fourth Gospel where the idea of a time "not yet come" appears. In John 2:4, Jesus responds to his mother's request for a miracle by saying his *hour* had not yet come. In John 7:30 and 8:20, failed attempts to seize Jesus are explained with the same phrase: "his hour had not yet come." In the other Gospels, Jesus often asks the beneficiaries of his miracles not to tell anyone. We can therefore conclude that John 7:1–14, as part of a larger group of passages, is talking about timing and not about a general strategy of secrecy. Jesus' use of secrecy was a matter of *timing*, not of *lifestyle*.

In the particular case of John 7:14, Jesus delayed only a few days before making himself public. The text says he went up to the temple "halfway through the Feast," and the feast lasted only seven days (Lev 23:34). This short time period is in stark contrast to the decades spent with a hidden identity by workers who never intend that identity to become public. But this text does clearly show that there is a time and place for being evasive and that not every time or place is right for going public. It does not, however, support an ongoing approach involving a hidden identity.

Another reason why this passage should not be used to defend a hidden-identity approach is that Jesus faced a real threat to his life (John 7:1). Most practitioners of hidden-identity face a threat of deportation, not death. A threat of death certainly justifies temporary secrecy, and a temporary threat of deportation may also justify secrecy. But ongoing secrecy, as needed for a hidden identity, is not supported by this passage.[7] This is highlighted further when we keep John 7 in the context of the rest of the fourth Gospel, which we will see has a particular focus on truth. Truth is not the opposite of secrecy, but it does have implications for our practice of secret-keeping.

The simplest justifications of the hidden-identity approach need no appeal to Scripture, but rely on the value of discretion: not everything about us needs to be divulged to everyone. There is no reason to blurt out that which will be poorly received or misunderstood. One couple's experience seeking financial support illustrates this point. They were invited to share about their ministry with the outreach committee at a church that espoused a narrower theological framework than they themselves did. Eric, the husband, saw no need to get into theological issues unless the church committee themselves asked, but his wife Tina, in the interests of transparency, raised some questions with the committee members. The ensuing conversation led to a decision by the committee not to support Eric and Tina. Yet the church would not have objected to any of what the couple actually did or taught overseas. There was no need for Tina

---

7. If a situation is so bad that one must hide one's true identity over a long period of time, it may be better to change that identity. If the identity—for example, as a follower of Jesus—is something that cannot possibly be changed, then one must either leave or be prepared to entrust one's life to God and face what may come.

to bring up that theological question at all, since the committee members did not raise the matter themselves.

The trouble with discretion as a justification for secrecy is the fine line between discretion and fear. When we have a strong interest in continuing our presence in Almoria or continuing a friendship, we may not be able to distinguish fear from discretion. What seems like discretion to us may look like fear to others. In one restricted country, for example, sent ones took what they considered to be the path of discretion by avoiding activities that would get them in trouble with the authorities. A local believer, however, when asked what he had learned from expatriate brothers and sisters, gave a disheartening answer: he said that what he had noticed most was the foreigners' fear of losing their visas, which appeared to govern all their actions.

If we can be honest with ourselves, we will be able to recognize the difference between fear and discretion. If we are incapable of being honest with ourselves, we can ask God to reveal to us how much of our motive is discretion, and how much is fear. We may also benefit from the insights of Almorian friends, if they can be persuaded to speak openly. The concern for keeping doors open is a valid one, but preservation of our visa status should never be our primary consideration. Discretion is a good motivation; fear is not.

A further justification, based more or less on common sense, goes as follows: "The Almorian secret police know who you are anyway and therefore you don't really need to hide anything, or you hide it just to prevent them from being embarrassed." Indeed, one should assume that any country's secret police know all they want to know about expatriates there. One can also assume that not every member of the secret police is zealously implementing stated government policies, and that not every member of government agrees with the general views of society. In other words, even if Almorian society and/or the Almorian government oppose the presence of missionaries, individual members of the secret police or foreign ministry may not. These officials may choose to ignore evidence that someone is a sent one (or avoid looking for evidence) as long as that person keeps a low profile. If, on the other hand, sent ones do or say things that publicly suggest a missionary identity, the relevant officials may be pressured to take action. That is, sent ones may be expelled if negative public attention is focused on the authorities' earlier lenience in letting them stay. For this reason, it is argued, sent ones should keep a low profile so the secret police aren't forced by other Almorians who object to their presence to expel them.

While all of that may be true, the justification fails at an important point: we do not *want* to live and act under cover. Not only is this what the secret police expect from foreigners, it is also too much like *their* way of doing things. Secret police are not the ones we want to emulate! *TIME* quotes a minister in Morocco as saying that some Christian workers "seem to have been inspired by the book of James, verse 007," referring to the fictional secret agent James Bond, code named 007 (Van Biema 2003:41). Why should there be a "cloak and dagger" approach to serving Jesus?

One might reply that there has to be a hidden-identity approach if an expatriate wishes to serve God in Almoria: all expatriate followers of Jesus who feel called by God to be in Almoria can be considered in some sense "sent ones," no matter how they are financed or how few ties they have to a sending organization or a sending church. Keeping quiet about this identity of "sent one," so the general wisdom goes, is the only way to serve Jesus in Almoria long term because it is the only way to *stay* in Almoria. This rationale assumes that it is completely impossible to publicly mention anything about one's calling or sending in Almoria. At the end of this chapter, I will call this assumption into question, but first let us look at further problems of a hidden identity.

EFFECTS OF HIDDEN IDENTITY ON RELATIONSHIPS

Phil, the business director mentioned in the Introduction, ran into an awkward situation with his management assistant, Radan, because he was trying to keep private the missional purpose of some expatriate colleagues. This attempt at concealment strained his relationship with Radan. The example illustrates the fact that a secret identity is not just something kept from officials in Almoria, but also from neighbors and colleagues and friends.

Every culture categorizes information into that which is normally kept private and that which is readily shared. In the United States, for example, people rarely ask someone how much they earn, even if that person is a close friend. In many parts of Asia, however, that question is commonly asked when meeting someone for the first time. In authoritarian cultures, people may rarely speak of their political views, whereas in cultures where there is an open political climate anyone can express political opinions freely. Within a given culture, the amount of information shared depends on the closeness and nature of the relationship; generally speaking, more is shared within a close relationship than in a casual friendship or working relationship. This is not a hard and fast rule, of course. In many cultures husbands and wives share little with each other about their daily lives, each keeping his or her workday world apart from the other.

Regardless of how open or reserved a given culture might be, deliberately hiding what would normally be shared in a particular relationship will surely harm that relationship or limit its growth. Hiding information may be deemed necessary in various situations, but it always has a cost. First, if one party discovers what has been hidden, there is a sense of betrayal or disappointment. What is more, the calculation "Should I keep this information from my friend?" inserts an element of inequality to the relationship. People make this calculation all the time with children, and appropriately so: the relationship between adults and children is *not* one of equals, especially if the adult is the parent. Adults do need to keep some truths from young children—some of the truths about the evil in the world, for example—because the children are not ready to cope with all the facts. Children also tend not to keep secrets well, and it is wise to avoid giving them sensitive information.

When we hide the truth about our identity or our agenda from people we meet in Almoria, we create a barrier between them and us. No matter what may motivate us to withhold information from Almorian friends and acquaintances, doing so introduces an element of inequality to the relationship. We know something they don't know, something we want them never to know. Such inequality detracts from a relationship with Almorian friends and colleagues, if for no other reason than that it increases the distance between us and them. If we have a secret we absolutely must keep, then we have no choice; but it will affect the relationship, however imperceptibly at first. By the same token, our friends may well have their own secrets they are keeping hidden from us: for example, they may not have disclosed all their reasons for becoming our friends. What they withhold from us will also weaken the relationship.

The sense of betrayal that comes when someone discovers that they have not been told a relevant piece of information is not to be underestimated. Jack, an expatriate follower of Jesus in Almoria, resigned from his sending organization to avoid this problem, after starting a business with an Almorian partner. Jack knew that he could neither tell his business partner about the sending organization, nor accept the risk that his partner might find out about it through other channels. The sense of betrayal that the partner would have felt, had he found out, would have destroyed the relationship. Resignation from the sending organization was the only course open.

Jack could have told everything to his partner, but that was not the option he chose. Instead, he chose to remove the ongoing secret from his life. This choice suggests that it is not only keeping secrets that can hurt relationships: telling everything, especially in an untimely or insensitive manner, can also cause damage. Politeness and consideration are positive reasons for withholding information. If we feel people are uninterested in our secrets, we may not want to push information on them. Sharing something simply for the sake of transparency can seem unnatural, and artificially inserting some fact we feel obliged to include may even be rude in a particular conversation. Listening more than one talks is a good thing (Jas 1:19), and openness is not *always* beneficial to relationships, especially in high-context cultures where much is expressed without words.

Some people are comfortable keeping significant parts of their lives out of their interactions with friends and colleagues, and their relationships may not suffer from their reticence to share about themselves. Others are bothered by secrets, preferring complete transparency. But they may nevertheless keep their organizational and financial ties secret in Almoria because it seems the prudent choice for maximizing the length of their stay. Still others may keep their own information secret in order to honor the privacy of fellow inter-cultural workers. For example, some fear that if one's sending organization information became known, this could lead to trouble for all members of the sending organization in Almoria. Alternatively, workers may be concerned that if one member of a locally registered organization revealed links to a sending organization, this could lead to unwanted scrutiny for other members. Sometimes, we keep secrets from one friend in order not to betray another.

Those who value transparency should remember that although in some cultures such transparency in relationships is exalted as a virtue, in others it is denigrated as foolish or naïve no matter how close the relationship may be. Indeed, individuals and cultures vary a great deal in the extent to which self-disclosure is preferred or expected in relationships. While some value openness, others share only what is necessary to achieve their ends. Those who are bothered by secrets, however, often have the nagging feeling that if their Almorian friends or colleagues knew about their sending organization and funding sources, the welcome they have been given might be rescinded, in keeping with the prevailing negative view of missionaries in Almorian society.

Some sent ones suggest that keeping a hidden identity secret is not primarily about our own security but rather about the well-being of our Almorian friends and colleagues. If they should ever be called in for questioning by secret police, they would be spared the emotional turmoil of choosing between betraying us by giving information, and suffering the pain of whatever means police might use to extract information. The trouble with this argument is that although ignorance of our affairs may save our friends from the inconvenience of betraying us, it will *not* save them from the secret police's methods for getting what they want. Protestations of ignorance would probably be interpreted by authorities as a refusal to cooperate, and could lead to further difficulties that would far eclipse any emotional turmoil over questions of betrayal. If our concern is truly for our friends and not for our own security, we should ask them, right at the beginning of the friendship, how the Almorian security services look upon those who associate with foreigners. If we are truly concerned for our friends, and if we have the courage to raise the matter with them, we will let them be the ones to decide how much or how little information about us is good for them.

There is one piece of information, however, that is essential to share with new friends and colleagues, and even officials: the fact that we are followers of Jesus. For many of us, this is easier said than done. It is not that we are ashamed of Jesus, but we may feel it is unnatural, forced, or even rude to bring Jesus into a particular conversation. Failure to do so at the beginning makes it harder to do later, but knowing this does not usually help us. The more that Jesus is central to every part of our lives, the easier it will be to mention him when we talk about ourselves. When Jesus has changed your life, and you live each day filled with gratitude for what he has done, people will notice.

If we plan (or hope) to engage in any public religious activity in Almoria—such as preaching, leading worship, or hosting a Bible study—it is probably good to tell our Almorian friends and colleagues about the religious activities we engaged in at home, prior to coming to Almoria. This way, they should not be surprised if they learn we are doing similar things in Almoria. If they want to know more about our specific activities or planned activities, they can ask. Note that they may do so indirectly, particularly in cultures where indirect communication is the norm. One needs to be alert to this possibility.

In conclusion, one point remains to be made concerning the effects of a hidden identity on relationships: *everyone* has secrets and *no one* shares *everything* with anyone. Complete transparency is impossible. As the ethicist Sissela Bok says, "Human beings can be subjected to every scrutiny, and reveal much about themselves; but they can never be entirely understood, simultaneously exposed from every perspective, completely transparent either to themselves or to other persons" (1989a:21). In other words, even in a culture that values transparency, there is a limit to how much one reveals. Discretion is always called for when sharing anything with anyone. Just because something need not be hidden does not mean it should be broadcast to everyone. But the discretion we employ in choosing what to share with a new acquaintance, or with the official who is processing our visa application or work permit, is not the same as a calculated, long-term choice to hold back information from friends or colleagues. It is the long-term choice that can make trouble for relationships. Also, using our personal discretion about when to keep something private is not the same as doing so out of obligation. The former gives us the freedom to choose when to share, while the latter imposes the burden of keeping a secret.

THE PROBLEM OF CLASHING IDENTITIES

A missionary identity when raising support, and another identity when applying for a visa: the two can be kept apart only by withholding the missionary purpose from anyone connected with the visa purpose. In other words, keeping secrets will be necessary if one has a missionary identity, and as we have seen, this approach easily leads to "stretching the truth." For some, this may seem duplicitous; for others, simply practical. In this matter, there is a definite cultural variation. I have never met an Asian who was troubled by a dual or hidden identity—they see the formal identity as just that: a formality. They presume that the authorities are in fact aware of the supposedly hidden identity and they are happy to leave it at that. In high-context cultures (such as many Asian cultures), much is left unsaid for the sake of politeness. The only troubling thing about a hidden identity, for someone from a high-context culture, is that certain kinds of ministry must be avoided in order to maintain the formal identity.

There are also differences between modern and postmodern culture regarding multiple identities. Modernity frames multiple identities as a question of lack of integrity, or at the very least lack of consistency. Postmoderns, on the other hand, see differences in "self" as inherent in the different social and relational contexts within which the self exists. In a postmodern worldview, it would therefore be quite normal for one's "revealed" identity to vary from context to context. In point of fact, everyone has more than one "identity" because we all have multiple roles in our families, our occupations, and our leisure activities. It would be a rare thing for a person to present all their different identities at a first meeting with someone. For example, many people use different business cards depending on the context and the purpose for which they are presenting themselves.

But even though we each have many identities, whether or not we are Asian or postmodern, we will all have a problem if the identities clash. Consider a case reported in *The New York Times* article "Tales Told Out of School in Pyongyang Cause Stir" (Gladstone 2014). Suki Kim, a Korean-American author, worked as an English teacher at the Pyongyang University of Science and Technology in 2011. In order to get the job, she had agreed not to write about what she experienced. Yet she secretly noted interesting quotes and stories, successfully smuggled them out of North Korea, and published a book in 2014 using the material.

During her time in North Korea, Ms. Kim effectively concealed her identity as a clandestine book researcher under the guise of a compliant member of the university staff. When the book came out, however, the mask was removed and her former North Korean hosts, as well as her former employers, were shocked and betrayed. For her part, she felt badly about causing trouble, but considered it a small cost to pay for the opportunity to live in North Korea for an extended period as an undercover writer. Whether she wanted the opportunity purely for her own ambition, or whether she claimed some higher purpose in writing her book, makes no difference to those whom she deceived. Betrayal is betrayal, whatever the motive.

Ms. Kim, however, paints her former colleagues as the ones with clashing identities, arguing that their self-description as "educators" is merely a guise covering up their "true" identity as missionaries. The university president denies that charge, saying that North Korean authorities know they are Christian educators. Since the educational program they have promised is being delivered, he would say there is no clash of identities. So far, it would seem that the North Korean authorities agree. Ms. Kim's book has been a far greater concern to them than the question of the students' beliefs. But the story is far from over. Humanly speaking, the end of the story may well depend on how far up in the North Korean hierarchy the university staff's Christian character was known, and how successfully the university and the North Korean authorities can pin the "trouble" on Suki Kim. If she can be portrayed as the only one who has betrayed anyone's trust, the university may be able to continue business as usual (which it was still doing in late 2016).

This example from North Korea is a pertinent illustration of clashing identities, but in order to gain a deeper appreciation for how it feels to be betrayed, examples are needed from closer to home. Since I am unaware of any real examples, the following stories are fictional and hypothetical; even if they seem unlikely, they can help us feel what it is like for people in other cultures when a sent one comes with a hidden identity.

Imagine that someone joins your congregation, is baptized, becomes a member of your church, and takes full part in the life of the church over a period of two years. You are glad to have her as a fellow member. After the two years, she moves to another city and you lose touch. Later, you learn that she has published a book that is an ethnographic study of your church. You read the book and discover that her profession of faith, her baptism, membership, and all her activities were done purely for the sake of a cultural anthropologist's "participant observation." In fact, she was a faculty member of a liberal university in a faraway city during her whole time in your church. She was and is a committed atheist, and her research was motivated by a desire to portray evangelical Christianity as a hypocritical sham. How would you feel? Her two identities—committed church member and atheist anthropologist researcher—definitely clash.

Alternatively, imagine that someone joins your church, earns trust, and volunteers his time to help with the church youth ministry. He gives of himself wholeheartedly and is well-liked by all who know him. He is a great mentor for the youth. But a few years later, more and more of those young people seem to be losing their faith when they are in college. After some investigation, it comes to light that this man had in fact been sowing seeds of doubt all along in those he mentored. He had done it so skillfully that no one had noticed. But it had been deliberate. No one could be sure why, but far from intending to build up the youth in their faith, he had always intended to tear it down. When his hidden agenda was discovered, the church felt betrayed.

What can we learn from these stories, other than what it feels like when you learn that someone you thought you knew has another identity or agenda that clashes with the one you were familiar with? In all three stories, from the Suki Kim account to the hypothetical scenarios above, the betrayals involved falsification of membership criteria. A sent one might never falsify information on a visa application or work permit submission; but would the officials granting these permissions feel deceived if they later learned about the worker's sending organization and sources of financial support? Would they say that the workers' public and private identities clashed? As the *TIME* magazine article already mentioned, "Visa bans turn many Evangelicals, usually straightforward to a fault, into truth stretchers" (Van Biema 2003:41).

One might argue that government officials need never know of the worker's organizational links or funding sources; after all, unlike Suki Kim or our fictional anthropologist, the worker is not about to publish a book. Sympathetic Almorian officials themselves may suggest putting less on an application rather than more. For instance, a vice president of the Billy Graham Evangelistic Association was once advised by embassy staff from a restrictive country to put only the initials of his employer on his visa application (Wilson 1981:9). Yet, even if officials never find out, the clash of identities is known to the sent one and will affect him or her to one extent or another. Simply put, a missionary identity is prone to clash with a non-missionary work identity. Not surprisingly, people do best when their various identities are in harmony, not in conflict.

Consider some scenarios in which a potential clash of identities might be an issue. If you are applying for advanced study in a restrictive country, for example, do you mention the degree you have from a seminary? Can you cloak it in a non-provocative name like intercultural studies, or is it best to leave it out entirely? Would it have been better not to have it at all? But you cannot change the past! And what if you are writing an article about missions? Should you use a pseudonym? That has advantages, but once again it creates yet another identity.

Or what do you say when you write to friends who are not Almorian, especially if you are sending out a single letter to a large address list? How do you describe yourself and your activities? What do you include about your Almorian friends and colleagues? Would you show your letter to them? If not, think twice about what you are writing.

Clashing identities are also sensed by our children, who notice differences in the way we present ourselves in different contexts. Some children may not be bothered by such differences, but others will interpret the differences as duplicity on the part of their parents. People ministering to children of sent ones have expressed concern to me about parents who present different versions of themselves, one in their country of origin and one in Almoria. This disparity can lead to disillusionment with all that the parents stand for because the children perceive a lack of integrity. In at least one case, a worker's child who later rejected her parents' belief system made an explicit connection between that rejection and what she had perceived as duplicity in her parents' different presentations of themselves in different places. Other children might be infected with the fear of expulsion and carry their parents' hidden identity as a burden too heavy for their years. They know there are secrets to be kept, but like the eight-year-old boy who told his teacher his father was a missionary, many children cannot keep secrets.

The burden is not just felt by children. Rick Love, writing in the context of those serving among Muslims, says: "This dual identity results in low-grade anxiety for many who feel as though they are hiding their true identity and motives from their Muslim friends. They face the nagging fear that they may be found out. It also makes it hard for some cross-cultural disciple makers to maintain a clear conscience before God and man (cf. Acts 24:16). The result: lack of integrity and lack of boldness to share the gospel" (2008:34).

EFFECTS OF HIDDEN IDENTITY ON THE SECRET-KEEPER

A hidden identity can cause problems for the one hiding it in at least four ways other than the problems it causes for relationships, and the anxiety just mentioned. First, *a hidden identity may bring about unpleasant comparisons.* My wife vividly recalls a gathering that was organized for U.S. citizens living in a Central Asian city to meet with a visiting American Embassy official. One of the locally resident Americans had a markedly negative view of missionaries. "Have you ever seen a middle-aged man carrying a guitar on public transportation here?" he asked. "You can be sure he's a missionary. But he won't tell you he is. No, they are like cockroaches! They hide from the light and come out when they think no one is looking." It seemed an unfair comparison, and yet there are ways in which secretive behavior does approach that of a cockroach.

Second, *hiding one's identity wears a person down*, especially one who prefers transparency. Jon Freeman, who has worked in leadership development and starting fellowships, puts it this way: "For those who hold to a scrupulously high view of honesty, in which withholding part of the truth is tantamount to lying, living and ministering in a country closed to missionaries may seem to demand continual compromise of their ethical standards as they repeatedly withhold their ministry intentions from peers, government officials, neighbors, and friends" (2010:132). In fact, not many do have such a "scrupulous" view of honesty, since most acknowledge that withholding information can be acceptable at times. But it still can wear you down, particularly if you are a leader who is guarding the private identities of others, not just your own. Many feel that no honest person should ever have to wear a mask. One organization displayed the prevalence of this sentiment in its repeated discussions about identity. The essential question was, "Are we missionaries, or aren't we?" It was always answered in the negative ("We aren't"), but it was never answered conclusively. The question kept coming up. Presumably the members of the organization felt obligated to hide parts of their identity, but would have preferred not to do so.

Keeping quiet is a third way that a hidden identity can be a problem. By definition, one needs to keep quiet about a hidden identity. But keeping quiet in certain contexts easily leads to keeping quiet in general. One is always wondering whether saying something will result in trouble for oneself or others. This preoccupation leads some expatriate followers of Jesus in Almoria not to share Jesus at all.

Finally, another way that secrets affect their keepers lies in *the connection between secrecy and lying*. Although there is nothing dishonest about withholding information, Bok notes that secrecy and lying "intertwine and overlap." She explains: "Lies are part of the arsenal used to guard and to invade secrecy; and secrecy allows lies to go undiscovered and to build up." She goes on to say that "whereas every lie stands in need of justification, all secrets do not" (1989a:x). So although she would agree that keeping secrets from a government does not necessarily need justification, she also warns that doing so can easily lead to lying, which *does* need justification. And when it comes to lying, she says (in the context of telling a "small" lie),

> The most serious miscalculation people make when weighing lies is to evaluate the costs and benefits of a particular lie in an isolated case, and then to favor lies if the benefits seem to outweigh the costs. In so doing, they risk blinding themselves to the effect that such lying can have on their integrity and self-respect, and to the jeopardy in which they place others. (1999:xix)

So if followers of Jesus have secrets and end up bending the truth to keep them, it is not just a matter of whether or not that can be justified, it is something that affects both them and their relationships with others. Whether or not Christian workers are in fact being dishonest, others already have that perception. As *TIME* noted, "Muslim critics accuse missionaries of lying [to governments] about their identities and their faith to achieve their goals" (Van Biema 2003:38).

HONESTY AND INTEGRITY:
CONCLUDING THOUGHTS ON IDENTITY

Are sent ones lying, or are their critics overstating the case? This question, focusing as it does on defining the boundary between falsehood and truth, distracts us from the deeper question of how best to be people of truth. The following thoughts from ethicists

Glen Stassen and David Gushee help us to orient ourselves appropriately with regard to truth and falsehood.

First, Stassen and Gushee point to the centrality of truth and truthfulness in God's character: "Truthfulness rather than any kind of deceit is a characteristic of the inbreaking reign of God" (2003:377). They point out that truth is a characteristic of Jesus as portrayed in the Gospels, especially John's Gospel. He is "full of grace and truth" (John 1:14), and he is "the way, the truth and the life" (John 14:6). And in the Old Testament, "Hebrew words for 'truth' and 'truly' (*emeth* and *amen*), or phrases describing God as 'the God of truth' (Ps 31:5; Is 65:16; cf. Rev 15:3), point to God's reliability, fidelity and trustworthiness. It is not just that God speaks truth but that *God is true*" (2003:378, emphasis in original).

The subject of God's character begs a return to Jesus' teaching in Matthew 10:16 about shrewdness and innocence. How do these characteristics fit into God's character? If Jesus has told us to be shrewd, how does that relate to the reliability and trustworthiness that Stassen and Gushee are talking about? We do not normally think of a shrewd person as someone to be trusted, so how can a trustworthy God be shrewd? The answer lies in Jesus' combination of innocence with shrewdness: he has perfectly combined the two, and is perfectly trustworthy. He must be our only model. As our Savior and Lord he also empowers and enables us to become more like him.

Second, the Apostle John highlights the importance of truth in a believer's character. "Disciples are 'from the truth' (1 John 3:19) and 'in the truth' (2 John 1:1); the 'truth abides in [them]' ([2] John 1:2). They are made holy, or sanctified, in the truth (John 17:17)," write Stassen and Gushee (2003:378). Even if one reads "truth" in these verses as a veiled reference to Jesus himself, it is still emphasizing the "truth" aspect of Jesus' character. And, as the authors conclude, "participation in God's reign involves not just an individual reorientation but the creating and sustaining of a new kind of covenant community, the church, characterized in a pioneering way by the practice of truthful living and straightforward, yet loving, truth-speaking" (2003:380). Such a community cannot be created if its members keep secrets from one another.

We want to model truth and not deceit. Even in a case where one could argue for the benefit of lying (such as to save the life of an innocent person being hunted by enemies), ethicist Ronald Preston insists that "one has to be habitually truthful" to know when it might be time for an exception (1986:363). When one has a hidden identity, it is easy to become habitually deceitful in place of habitual truthfulness. This is especially true when one is in leadership of an organization and guarding the identity of others.

Fortunately, hidden identities are not necessary for sent ones in Almoria. As we will see, it is possible to cultivate an open identity that can be shared with anyone. This identity can be presented to like-minded evangelicals, to secular people hostile to missionary activity, and to anyone in Almoria. Rick Love calls this a "core identity":

> A core identity speaks of 'integrity' and 'integration'—words that come from the same Latin root: to make whole. Integrity refers to consistency between inner convictions and outward actions. We will be walking in integrity when we have 'truth in the innermost being' (Ps 51:6). Honesty, sincerity, lack of deceit, and guilelessness are other ways of describing it. We cannot continue to think of ourselves as missionaries in one context and aid workers, teachers or businessmen in another. This reflects not only a split personality but a split spirituality—a false understanding that spiritual aspects of our life or our work are more important than the practical parts of life. (2008:35)

In Love's conception, being a "sent one" is an integral part of a sent one's core identity. Love says that "our motivation, our tentmaking role, our personal gifting, and our apostolic calling" should all be aligned and working together.[8] "In other words," he continues, "moved by the love of Christ, we seek tentmaking opportunities that fit who God has made us and allow us to carry out our apostolic calling with full integrity. If we have an integrated identity, then it will be natural for us to share our faith with greater freedom and boldness" (2008:35). When keeping secrets, it is harder to experience such freedom or boldness.

How is it possible to have an open "apostolic calling" or identity of "sent one" in a restrictive country, one might ask. We will consider that question in a moment. I argue that it *is* possible to have a single identity that encompasses all of who you are and is recognizably the same in any context. Or, if one takes the view that everyone has multiple identities in any case, it is possible for these identities not to clash with each other, and for none to require hiding. It is possible to be recognizably *one person* in every context.

Some have argued that the identity one is sent with can be different from the identity one is received with, and that this is understandable to anyone. "Sent as a missionary, received as an engineer," for example: two different identities for two very different places. It might be ideal to keep your missionary identity private in Almoria so as to save face for officials who turn a blind eye to what they know about it—this is the rationale for the hidden-identity approach. But links between the two places are hard to avoid: in today's interconnected world it may be impossible to prevent people in Almoria from seeing the identity you were sent with. There might be something on a church website or in a letter or e-mail; there might well be a visitor from Almoria in your home town, not to mention whatever might slip out if someone from your sending church visits you in Almoria. And even if you successfully avoid all of these and other potential links (such as social media), there is one link you cannot avoid: you and your family. You and your family

---

8. In speaking of "apostolic calling," Love is using the word apostolic in the sense of "pertaining to a sent one" (from the Greek *apostello*, meaning to send).

members may succeed in keeping your hidden identity private but, as we have seen, this success carries its own consequences.

The bottom line about identity—whether a person has one or many—is that one's visible identity or identities should match one's stated identity. If there is any disconnect between what one states and what others observe, this will be obvious; and a good reputation gained in the community could be lost instantly. We must be who we say we are! This means our self-descriptions should match our actual actions. It means that what we say about ourselves in one group should be recognizably similar to what we say in a totally different group with different values. It means that our funding sources should also match what we say about ourselves (although sources of funding need not be disclosed unless required by law).

We must be men and women of integrity, through and through. Rather than a church-planting team being clothed in the garb of "business people" or "NGO workers," genuine business people or development workers should be prepared to go as genuine kingdom people. Whether they end up planting a church or not is another matter; what I am emphasizing here is that they be true to their advertised identity. Remember that service or work can be done for its own value to God, not merely for creating opportunities to transmit a spoken message calling people to follow Jesus.

MODIFYING THE MISSION TO AVOID HIDDEN IDENTITY

Since service in itself has value, perhaps churches should add the category of "service" to their sending. The church could still send "missionaries" to unrestrictive countries, but would send workers to Almoria for "service" instead, so that those sent to Almoria can have the same public identity in their home churches as in Almoria. And because the public identity and purpose would be the same in all places, there would no longer be any need for a hidden identity.

Being sent for service instead of for evangelism or church planting does not prevent someone from sharing the good news; evangelism and church planting simply become *private* rather than public purposes. The private purpose is kept private *everywhere*—not only in Almoria. The publicized purpose is the same in all places.

In order for a private purpose to be private everywhere, one has to ensure that it is spoken of only in venues where every person present (as distinct from everyone who was invited) is personally known by either the speaker or the organizer of the event. This may be inconvenient for the hosts and organizers, but the consequences can be potentially devastating, as some expatriate followers of Jesus in a restrictive Asian location discovered.

The group had gathered to pray for their city. They did not all know each other, and there were Asian as well as Western expatriates present. So no one took special notice of a certain Asian man sitting quietly at the back—until a point in the meeting when two men began leading the group in prayer. The man at the back then stood up and identified himself as the local representative of the government's Council for Religious Affairs. He announced that those leading the prayer would need to leave the country for having engaged in unauthorized religious activity.

Such surprises are not limited to restrictive countries. In Mitt Romney's 2012 U.S. presidential campaign, an "off-the-record" speech at a private fundraiser was taped by a bartender working at the event and then released nationwide to the detriment of Romney's presidential hopes. This outcome could possibly have been avoided had the organizer made certain that all those present were personally known—not just those on the guest list. One way a sent one can be confident about a meeting's privacy is by holding private gatherings only in people's homes.

Because of the difficulty of keeping a purpose private, it may be best to choose a public purpose that can incorporate the good news in a way that "service" probably cannot. What we need is a genuine and holistic purpose that incorporates both word and deed in a way that lets Almorian officials see us as we truly are: people who genuinely seek to bless their country. Rick Love has advocated the use of "blessing the nations" as a framework (2008:34). This concept begins with the promise of God to Abraham that "all peoples on earth will be blessed through you" (Gen 12:3). Christopher J. H. Wright traces the blessing of the nations throughout the Bible in his book *The Mission of God*. The greatest blessing of all is the restoration of relationship with God through faith in Christ, but this is not the only blessing God endows. Many people need to see God's love demonstrated in tangible ways before they can begin to think about the importance of Christ to their relationship with God. Using the "blessing the nations" approach, then, means that all aspects of intercultural outreach are explained in terms of the blessing they bring to the nations.

Another holistic approach to the outreach of God's people is that of "dignification," to use a term from missiologist Jayson Georges. As Georges points out, all of Jesus' ministry can be seen as restoring dignity to those whose lives he touched, through miracles, healings, and deliberate interaction with the downtrodden. "His miraculous healings and radical table fellowship restored dignity and honor to marginalized people," writes Georges (2014:39). Jesus' death and resurrection covered shame and restored honor to us in our relationship to God. God's salvation throughout the Old Testament also shows the marks of dignification, and our work can do so as well. All of the church's outreach, for that matter, can be described in terms of dignification. As Georges puts it, "In the epistle to the Romans, salvation is not simply forgiveness of sins, the imputation of alien righteousness, or eternity in heaven, but honor and glory, the removal of shame, and group inclusion" (2010:301).

It is not my purpose to recommend one specific approach or metaphor over another, but rather to suggest that any metaphor in today's interconnected world needs to be suitable for discussion in any context and in anyone's presence. Even if we are able to keep our private purposes private everywhere, we do much better to have a purpose that need not be hidden. It may not be easy to find such a metaphor for universal use, but it can be done and it is well worth the effort.

Metaphors that can be used anywhere are nevertheless used differently in different places. In a home church, the congregation needs to understand why they would want to support you; in Almoria, officials need to know why they would want you in their country. In the home church, the metaphor helps people to understand why they should care about outreach in general, and your work in particular; in Almoria, the metaphor helps an official understand what you plan to do in Almoria. For example, when speaking to your church, you might describe how Jesus brought dignity to all those he ministered to, and suggest that we should bring dignity too. You might then describe how your work in Almoria fits the approach of dignification. With an Almorian official, you could also mention that Jesus brought dignity, and therefore you do too. In our interconnected world, the Almorian official may find you linked to your church on the internet in one way or another. Before she does, it may be good to explain to her that your church *also* supports dignification, so much so that they have contributed financially to your work. The value of the dignification metaphor is that it works in both places and is recognizable as the same in both, even though you use it differently in your home church than you do in Almoria. For the church, Jesus' action legitimizes yours; for the official, dignification is its own legitimacy.

If you used a more traditional metaphor, however, things would be different. In church, you could begin with the fact that Jesus calls us to make disciples of all nations, so we also need to do that. You could then tell how your work in Almoria helps you to make disciples and therefore, by extension, helps the church to do so. But if you used this metaphor with the Almorian official, you almost certainly would find yourself on the next flight home. Unless that official was the one in a hundred (or a thousand) who wanted to become a disciple of Jesus, you and your disciple-making plans will be entirely unwelcome in Almoria.

In choosing a metaphor, one needs to think about the different places where it might be used:

- in churches
- in a sending organization (for example, in a vision or mission statement)
- on a visa application (although it may be best not to use an outreach or disciple-making metaphor here, but instead to stick with better-known categories related to one's proposed area of work)
- on a work permit application (here also, it may be better to use already-known categories)
- in registering an organization or a business
- in a resume or job application

What or how much should be shared or publicized differs from case to case. But in all cases, secrecy leads us in the wrong direction. Secrecy and discretion are not the same. Although they may overlap, secrecy carries a connotation of more serious consequences in the case of a breach of confidence. Discretion, on the other hand, is simply the wise response in a particular case; and a breach of discretion has less serious consequences. Nevertheless, neither discretion nor secrecy should lead us to habitually avoid revealing our identity as followers of Jesus who desire to honor Jesus in everything. The more often that one can be upfront and open with people about being a follower of Jesus, the more likely it is that such conversations will occur again.

As we have seen, it is not Jesus who causes us to keep our metaphors secret, but the metaphors themselves that are faulty. Such metaphors should therefore be discarded in favor of new metaphors that do not cause unnecessary offense. Consider how a revised metaphor could be used in the case of an expatriate, Bella, applying for the position of Vice President for Academic Affairs at the English University of Almoria. The existing metaphors of conversion or church planting would cause a problem: if the university human resources department googled Bella and found her on her church's missions page, the Vice President job would surely go to someone else. On the other hand, if the university found Bella on a webpage—even a church page—promoting mutual inter-action and learning between faiths, this discovery would not present a problem. It might even strengthen Bella's application, especially if Bella *herself* had mentioned her desire for interfaith dialogue *before* her potential employer found evidence of it on the internet.

New metaphors have to be adopted not only at the intellectual level but also at the heart level. The change cannot be in name only. In other words, to use the metaphor of interaction and mutual learning mentioned above, one really needs to believe deeply in the benefits of such interaction in order to adopt this metaphor and not just use it as a cover for some other "real" purpose. Indeed, along with changing how we talk about our purpose, we must also make our "walk" match our talk. A truly new metaphor must transform not only our words, but our actions as well; otherwise, the new metaphor is no more than a new name for the old hidden purpose. "Blessing the nations," for example, means spending at least as much time in doing good deeds as in saying good words. The recipients of our outreach may need to feel blessed in the here and now before they will accept a message about blessings pertaining to the hereafter.

The metaphor of dignification also has clear implications for our walk. Every activity or project should promote the dignity of those it touches and should cultivate a healthy sense of honor based on each person's value as someone created in God's image. Such projects could include helping the local economy, attending to the margin-alized, or providing opportunities for youth to develop a healthy identity. These activities connect directly with the dignifying message of Jesus and therefore provide an unforced opportunity to share the message of how Jesus restores our lost dignity before God.[9]

---

9. For more suggestions regarding dignification, see Chapter 4 of *The 3D Gospel: Ministry in Guilt, Shame, and Fear Cultures* by Jayson Georges (Self-published, 2014, pp. 65-71; locations 907-930 in Kindle edition). Also

Another new metaphor worth mentioning, even though it sounds trite, is simply to be who we are, wherever we are. Ever since the original "scattering" of the Jerusalem church in the first century (Acts 8), ordinary followers of Jesus have carried the good news of our Lord with them wherever they have gone. This is still the case today: diaspora and migrant-worker populations are larger than ever before, and tens of thousands of others are sent overseas by their employers. Among these varied groups of "accidentally sent" ones are many followers of Jesus.

In God's economy there is no "accident" in their sending. In fact, "intentional" sending by churches and sending organizations should be undertaken with great humility because it is only a small part of what God is doing in the world. Intentional efforts carried out with appropriate humility can help equip the "accidental" workers who find themselves far from their homelands. Such efforts also have an important part to play in outreach to diaspora or migrant groups who do *not* know Jesus, right in the places where we live. Because such people often stay within their own groups, getting to know them and serving them often calls for intentionality and creativity. That subject is outside the scope of this book, but those of us who are called to remain at home must reach out to the foreigners in our cities, and we can trust God to give us all that is required for the task.

Some may doubt whether it is possible to mention that one's purpose includes serving Jesus and still be accepted into Almoria. Others may question the possibility of modifying one's mission as we have discussed, without diluting it beyond recognition by removing essential parts. Still others may object that the lives of Almorian followers of Jesus could be put at risk because of our mentioning Jesus. These are valid questions, and I believe they must be addressed.

---

see *Cross-Cultural Conflict* by Duane Elmer (Downers Grove, IL: InterVarsity Press, 1993).

First let me say that these potential concerns for Almorian believers apply to a small minority of cases. Anyone who has spent any length of time as a sent one in Almoria knows this. Even so, if there *is* a credible likelihood of local believers' lives being endangered by what expatriates say or do, then that is a strong reason to temper our statements or behavior. It is not for *us* to decide that *others* should lay down their lives—that is their choice to make.

As for the risk of expatriates not being admitted to Almoria, there are very few places where any mention at all of Jesus would result in denial of entry. If we are seeking entry to such a place, this is a risk we will need to take. It is also a risk we can significantly reduce by choosing a purpose that neither poses an obvious threat to local authorities and structures nor approaches them with the condescension often found in representatives of wealthy, "advanced" nations. Such an inoffensive purpose may indeed be seen by some followers of Jesus as "diluted." Yet, in our definition of "dilution," let us not uncritically accept old assumptions, but rather let us be confident that what we consider "essential" is indeed so.

PROS AND CONS OF A NEW METAPHOR

A new metaphor for outreach can address more than just the problem of a hidden identity. It can also prevent serious misunderstandings that arise from some of our present metaphors. These may be drawn from the language of conquest (e.g., "taking the nations for Jesus") or the language of condescension often used by colonial rulers (e.g., references to "dark" places, as if these places exist only in lands other than our own). Or the metaphors may be taken from the language of commerce, creating the impression of a contest of rivals competing for the same "customers." Consider the following excerpt about metaphors, from a statement published by the AD2000 & Beyond evangelistic movement:

We regret that certain words and images long employed to call the church to mission have increasingly caused offense to the very people with whom we are seeking to share the Good News. Some of these words and images are biblical; some are motivational tools from the secular arena that we use to inspire involvement and action. Many are military in nature: "target," "conquer," "army," "crusade," "mobilize," "beachhead," "advance," "enemy," "battle."

We may know what such terms mean to us, but what do they mean to others? Are we unintentionally making those we most want to befriend feel we regard them as enemies, while helping opponents of Christian mission to make their case against us? Can we find more reconciling, redemptive words and images in Scripture and elsewhere that will aid us in expressing love, respect and effective witness for Christ, rather than creating an atmosphere of adversarial confrontation? (2000)[10]

In point of fact, it is not only potential friends or opponents who may misunderstand the intent of our metaphors. We ourselves— probably without realizing it—may internalize the metaphors of conquest, colonialism, or commerce, as if they referred to cultural, religious, or national triumph rather than to spiritual influence. As we have seen, the Bible provides plenty of alternative ways to talk about the outreach of the people of God, metaphors that can replace those that cause unnecessary offense or lead us into unhelpful misunderstandings.

---

10. The entire text of the statement is reproduced in the Appendix. Note that the actual number of biblical passages using a military metaphor for outreach is smaller than one might imagine from the extent to which such metaphors have been used in the promotion of mission work.

Jesus' victory over the powers of darkness—to isolate that particular theological theme—has nothing to do with whether our country, our culture, or even our values or our religion (as an organized entity) is more successful than others. The lordship of Jesus is at home and yet a stranger in every culture, *including our own*. People in any culture can follow Jesus, but when there is a clash between Jesus' teaching and a particular cultural value, Jesus' followers must conform to him and not to their culture. And every culture—including that of the sent one—has facets that clash with Jesus' teaching, both blatantly and in subtle ways. We will never be free of cultural baggage in this life, but the more we can be aware of it and minimize it, the better.

Unfortunately, the cultural superiority and triumphalism that are "baggage" to us in Almoria can feel like "comfortable furniture" in our home church. Old, familiar ways of speaking and writing are easier for people to understand than new metaphors, which may only confuse the supportive members of a church who have come to hear about your ministry. More and more, however, congregations are *already* using new terminology for outreach as part of the hidden-identity approach. Church leaders may be reluctant to make yet another change in the language of outreach—especially if some feel it omits "essential" concepts. But they can be persuaded, even if doing so requires a full discussion of the problems of the hidden-identity approach. People can intuitively sense that the way of Jesus, although it certainly has a place for discretion and careful timing in the sharing of information, is not inherently about hiding one's identity.

In summary, the best way for a sent one to avoid a hidden identity in Almoria is to adapt purpose, metaphor, and motivation such that nothing needs to be hidden. This adaptation has to be at heart level, not merely on the surface. Further, to avoid hiding one's connections to a home church and/or sending organization, one must ensure that these groups have also implemented the new metaphor. However, even at this stage, when nothing *needs* to be hidden, it is still wise to use discretion when preparing written documents or formal applications, even though one *need not* hide anything. Visa or work permit applications and organizational registration documents may not be the place to announce one's allegiance to Christ or one's desire to serve him. It is ultimately in one's *relationships with people* where following Jesus needs to be spoken of. Thus, if including one's full purpose, outreach metaphor, or motivation in written documents or formal applications will help one to bring Jesus into conversations, then there may be a reason to include those details. Otherwise, it may be best to leave them out.

In closing this chapter, I must acknowledge that neither modifying one's mission nor adopting a new metaphor will completely remove all tensions from a sent one's life. Not every tension can be resolved. And if life had no tensions, where would be the necessity for faith in God on a daily basis? People in intercultural settings are faced with extra tensions because of living in another culture, and they need to find their way to a sufficient degree of peace to function in that context. As Jon Freeman puts it, "Tolerance for ambiguity . . . is important for arriving at or maintaining inner shalom" (2010:146). We cannot expect all ambiguity to disappear, no matter how much we change ourselves or modify our mission. However, if we can be open and avoid secrets, we will significantly reduce the ambiguity and anxiety that we face.

STEPS FOR ACTION, REFLECTION, AND GROUP DISCUSSION

1. Can you think of a time when you felt betrayed at having learned of someone's hidden identity or hidden agenda? How do children feel if they discover two clashing identities in a parent? Given the difficulty of keeping a private purpose private, and of keeping a missionary identity secret, is it not better to have a genuine identity that can be publicized anywhere?

2. Do you agree that secrecy can easily lead to lying? If not, does secrecy move us from being habitually truthful towards being deceitful? If it does, is there anything that could justify such a move?

3. Do you see any need to modify the metaphors used for outreach by followers of Jesus? Are there problems with metaphors of conquest, colonialism, or commerce—or are they always acceptable because they can be found in Scripture? Do they cause unnecessary misunderstandings or are such misunderstandings an inevitable result of spiritual battle? Can our metaphors mislead us from our true purpose? Which of the suggested modified metaphors, if any, seems best to you (service, blessing the nations, dignification, just being oneself, mutual interaction and learning—or one that was not suggested)?

4. Should an outreach metaphor be "suitable for discussion in any context and in anyone's presence?"

5. If new metaphors are needed, how can churches be persuaded to use them? How can the change become a heart-level change, not just a change of words?

6. What aspects of our culture need to be transformed by the lordship of Jesus? (I mean the culture of evangelicals, not of the wider society!) If you can't think of anything, find someone from another culture (possibly someone from your own country but who is not an evangelical) and ask them their opinion on this.

PART
TWO

PRACTICAL SUGGESTIONS

CHAPTER THREE
PREPARATION

Listen, learn, and understand; have the humility
of a guest and the commitment of a citizen.

How can a new metaphor for intercultural outreach be implemented in real life by someone seeking to serve in Almoria, or by someone already serving there with a hidden identity but working for an integrated one? Ideally, sending organizations would tailor their mission statements to the most restrictive of their focus groups, as we discussed in the preceding chapter, so that nothing would need to be hidden. This is an unlikely outcome at present, but there is another option: those called to Almoria may choose not to join any sending organization.

Not joining a sending organization has its own challenges. If one takes that path, one avoids the hidden identity that comes with most sending organizations, but one also misses out on the many services and supports provided by an organization. This part of the book focuses largely on how to do without these benefits. However, since not everyone can take an independent path, we will also consider suggestions for workers who choose to be part of an organization but who nevertheless seek to minimize hidden identity.

Since sending organizations connect with workers from before they start intercultural service all the way through the time of retirement, this section will also cover that full range. Included here are issues concerning the research phase of examining options, as well as longer-term issues concerning finances, non-financial support, and other matters such as children's education and retirement.[11] One's first days in a country set the pattern for the entire

---

11. Many good books have been written on these topics. Nearly all of them are written from the traditional approach of joining a sending organization,

time there, so it is important to think about all of these questions before leaving home.

PRELIMINARY QUESTIONS

Anyone seeking to serve interculturally has at least two preliminary questions to ask: *Who am I?* and *Where do I belong?* The two are related and should be answered together, not prioritized one over another. The first refers to the vocational side of one's core identity, in the sense of each individual's particular mix of gifts, skills, interests, and abilities. The second refers to place of service, people-group focus, and specific role. To prioritize the question of identity over where one belongs may place too much importance on the sent ones instead of on the people to be served. If, on the other hand, priority is placed on the place or people being served—for example, by looking for the place with the greatest need—one will probably end up doing something simply because there is a demand for that work in a needy place, instead of doing what God is calling one to do. In the early stages of service, such a choice may be fine, but in the long run, a role that is inconsistent with one's vocation leads to frustration and possibly even burnout.

FINDING A SUPPORT GROUP THAT SHARES YOUR CALLING

Before we discuss vocation, another matter needs to be addressed. Following Jesus is not a solo venture, and following Jesus to Almoria is all the more a group undertaking. This is why you should form a support group from the very beginning, even before you are sure of your vocation.

---

or they are about cross-cultural adjustment from a purely secular perspective. My father's book *On Being a Missionary* is in the former category (Pasadena: William Carey Library, 1995; updated edition 2012 by Thomas Hale and Gene Daniels).

If you do not know anyone who could be part of your support group, pray for connections. Connections can be made in unexpected ways. For instance, my parents met as partners in Anatomy Lab in medical school and then discovered they had similar life goals. One way that God confirms his call is by bringing you into contact with a small group of people who are excited by your calling. They may be scattered in different places, and they may have differing degrees of interest, but they will be prepared to support you—even financially, if necessary.

Your support group's role in helping you to serve in Almoria is a calling and a commitment on their part. Beyond their initial support and encouragement as you explore your calling, their help is needed in a variety of ways. For one thing, numerous tasks must be done in your home country while you are away. Even if you are ultimately seeking citizenship in Almoria, you will still have connections in your home country. You may also have legal obligations, such as filing of home-country tax returns or other financial concerns. All of the tasks together amount to more than what one person can do, so you will need to find a number of people to help you. One may be able to help with taxes, another with sending newsletters, and so on. If you cannot find the people you need, you may be able to set up a contractual arrangement with a sending organization to perform some of these services for a fee, without your being an actual member (assuming that you have chosen not to be).

FINDING YOUR VOCATION AND BEING WHO YOU SAY YOU ARE

In the traditional sending paradigm the question *Who am I?* had an obvious answer for sent ones: "I am a missionary." Some were missionary *doctors* or missionary *teachers*, but the *missionary* identity was preeminent and unquestioned. Today, however, as we have seen, service in Almoria does not usually permit a "missionary" identity unless it is hidden. Sent ones who seek to avoid a hidden identity need to find ways to be sent by Jesus to Almoria without being "missionaries." A different vocational identity needs to replace the missionary identity.

For many of us, finding this vocation is not easy. We may have numerous different interests, or we may have no idea what we do best. And it is not just young people who face this dilemma; many others have gone from one job to another without ever needing a firm answer to the *Who am I?* question. Or perhaps they never had time to answer the question. Before seriously considering service in Almoria, be sure to set aside time to reflect on the ways you have seen God use you.[12] Feedback from family, friends, and colleagues is also essential. Do not try to do this alone. While you may not reach a definitive answer, the clearer you can be about who you are called to be, the better. Knowing who you are does not mean you then refuse any role that matches you less than perfectly, but knowing yourself can help keep you from a completely mismatched role.

Closely related to the question of vocation is that of purpose. Is your purpose for going to Almoria one you could share freely with Almorian neighbors, colleagues, or officials? If your purpose centers on converting people to Christianity, then you could not share it widely without being asked to leave Almoria. The question is: does the Bible require you to convert people? In answering this question, we should note that the word "convert" appears only rarely in the New Testament. It never appears as an active verb, in the sense of someone converting someone else. Jesus called people to repentance, and he called his followers to make disciples, not converts. That may seem like an insignificant distinction, and an Almorian official would not be likely to see any difference between making converts and making disciples of Jesus. But finding the distinction is important in and of itself because it is good to search

---

12. A good place to start would be by reading J. Robert Clinton's books: *The Making of a Leader* (NavPress, 2012), *Unlocking Your Giftedness* (Barnabas, 1993), and *Focused Lives* (Barnabas, 1995) and its companion *Strategic Concepts that Clarify a Focused Life* (Barnabas, 1995).

the Scriptures ourselves in response to the tensions we encounter in life. The tension will never completely go away, but God will reveal to us the direction he wants us to take, as we seek him and search the Scriptures.

The finer points of definitions, or small differences between words, are not what is important. The important thing is the process of wrestling with Scripture to search for ways to be both faithful to Scripture and also transparent with the people around us. The brief discussion of conversion and disciple-making in the paragraph above illustrated that process. Being "faithful to Scripture" requires us to carefully sort out what is scriptural from what is cultural, or from that which is merely the result of historical precedent. The way that we read Scripture is deeply conditioned by culture and by tradition, so it is no small task to separate these as we seek to revise our purpose.[13]

Remember that this purpose is neither a "platform" nor a cover. If you went to Almoria as an English teacher, *be* an English teacher—not a missionary posing as an English teacher or an English teacher using that role to do other things not normally associated with teaching. If you started out with a purpose that is unacceptable to the Almoris, you will have to go through a period of transformation where you come to own your new purpose as yours, not just as a façade. This change will require time and prayer, and your support group will be key partners for working through the process with you.

Whatever you decide about your vocation and purpose, resolve to be who you say you are. No matter how you describe yourself, your actions tell people who you really are. For example, a university dean in Asia drew a distinction between Christian teachers who were clearly there to teach, and others for whom the role of teacher was merely a path for inviting students to meetings outside class

13. For help sorting out the scriptural from the cultural, see *Misreading Scripture with Western Eyes* by Randolph E. Richards and Brandon J. O'Brien (IVP, 2012).

time. The dean allowed the latter teachers to continue because of the students' need for interaction with native speakers, but she longed for more of the first kind. In the secular world of ESL, according to one person I talked with, Christian groups for whom teaching—and teaching well—is a core part of who they are stand out from those for whom English teaching is just a way to get a visa.

Remember that the vocational identity you want may not be available in Almoria. It may be entirely unheard of, or it may be restricted to Almorian citizens. As intercultural consultant Juha Jones points out, everyone entering a society "negotiates" a role there, and Almoria "may not have or allow the role you want" (2013). Ultimately, Almorian neighbors, friends, and colleagues will place you in one or more of their categories; in Jones's words, society "allocates" your role. What you say—or even what you do—may make little difference if Almorians have preconceived ideas about you. In many restrictive countries, foreigners are automatically placed in the category of spy; nothing you say or do can change that. A category I often found myself in as an English teacher was that of Peace Corps volunteer. In my first year of teaching, I took pains to ensure that people learned the name of the organization I actually worked for. But after hearing someone I had corrected a month earlier telling someone else, yet again, that I was a Peace Corps volunteer, I gave up on corrections and settled for the tame response of "Something like that" whenever I was miscategorized.

What if "who you are" is, at the end of the day, "missionary" and nothing else? What if there is no other profession with which you identify? For example, if your primary calling is Bible distribution, this is clearly against the law in many places. If it is important to you to be in Almoria long term with such a calling, then you will either have to live with a high degree of secrecy or have to have a very strong faith in God's ability to keep you in a place where the authorities don't want you. Sent ones called primarily to "full-time" ministry may in fact find no legitimate long-term residential role in Almoria. If you do find a way to live there, you may need to be prepared for a shorter stay than what you had initially planned! In some places, you can go in and out of the country on repeated tourist visas. While some workers adapt to such a lifestyle, others find it excessively disruptive (not to mention expensive). In any case, your stated identity in Almoria will be a matter of formality; you can divulge your unstated identity to those whom you trust, and ask them to keep it unstated as well. If you can keep your unstated identity unstated in your home country as well as in Almoria, you may avoid unwanted publicity in Almoria. Still, the difficulty of keeping something unstated cannot be overestimated. And an approach that requires an "unstated" identity is, of course, precisely the hidden-identity approach we have been seeking to avoid. There is no other option for those whose vocation is "missionary and nothing but missionary."

FINDING "YOUR" PEOPLE AND LEARNING HOW BEST TO SERVE THEM

We now come to the question *Where do I belong?* As noted already, this question is not necessarily secondary to *Who am I?* It can be answered in a number of ways, none of which has an inherent "rightness" relative to the others. Each worker is led differently. For many, a subjective sense of calling is of primary importance: "God called me to the Almori people," they will say. The *way* in which God calls, however, is not always subjective but may take a more objective or analytical form. For example, one line of argument suggests that the neediest group is the one that deserves the attention. If "need" is defined in terms of numbers of followers of Jesus, then the groups with the fewest followers are the ones to focus on. Since every country now has at least a few followers of Jesus, focus has shifted to "people groups," whether these be "unreached," with fewer than some set percentage of their people following Jesus, or whether they are "unengaged," because no followers of Jesus are intentionally seeking to reach them.

A quite different definition of "need" focuses on where current responsiveness to Christ is greatest. It suggests that workers are needed most where the "harvest is plentiful" (Matt 9:37). Yet another definition looks at physical needs and chooses the poorest people (or least educated, least served by medical care, etc.) as the ones most worthy of attention. Finally, one may focus less on the needs than on what one can offer. Such a focus leads to the place where one's vocation is most relevant.

In this regard, one needs to ask if the best use of one's vocation is not in one's own country. Will your vocation actually add value for Almoria, or is it already being done just as well or better by the Almorians themselves? You may make a case for working alongside them, but your ideas and experience may not automatically transfer to the Almorian context. There may indeed be a great need among the Almoris, but you may not be the one to meet it.

It may seem surprising that I would raise these questions here, but you may be able to do more to introduce Jesus to the Almoris by staying in your own country than by living in Almoria yourself. First of all, there may be Almoris living in your country, whether as immigrants, migrant workers, or international students. It may be more important for you to find them and reach out to them than to move to Almoria.[14] Second, you may have skills or connections that can be best used for the Almori people from outside their country. Such service could include organizing, recruiting, or coordinating the work of others, or even lobbying your government or serving in the capacity of peacemaker if relations are strained between your country and Almoria. Investigate what is being done along these lines before making plans to move to Almoria.

How are we to know which path to take—to go or not to go? First, we need humility: we need to exercise "sober judgment" when

---

14. Consider here the ministry of MoveIn (www.movein.to).

thinking of ourselves (Rom 12:3), and this means being realistic about our abilities and skills. Next we must look at the situation as objectively as possible. Are there signs that a different person would be more suitable, or that a different time would be better? Remember that God's call to a particular place always includes the particular time and specific mode of going—although these pieces may not come simultaneously with the original call. Sometimes you may need to wait a long time for these "further instructions." But God's timing is an integral part of his calling. And we must never forget that even though God calls us, our particular service is not indispensable. God has been at work already and will continue to be at work long after we are gone. This humility is essential as we fulfill our callings. When we are humbly confident of God's particular leading, we can move ahead with wisdom and boldness.

QUALIFICATIONS AND CROSS-CULTURAL TRAINING

Everyone needs to prepare. Even when Paul was rushing to Macedonia, the NIV says he and his team "got ready" (Acts 16:10). Although most other translations render a sense of seeking or trying rather than of preparation in this verse, preparation is nonetheless part of any endeavor. In Acts 16:10, whatever preparation Paul made was done "at once" and was surely not a cross-cultural training course. But it was preparation nonetheless. And we also need to prepare in many ways for intercultural service.

When you do have confidence that it is right to move to Almoria, the next step is to learn more about the Almori people. To find out about their worldview and beliefs, you may not need to go any farther than your own home town. There may not be Almoris there, but there may be others of the same or similar faith as the Almoris. Instead of going to a university or seminary to take a course on their religion, find out if there is a place of worship from that faith located near you. They may not have formal courses, but someone will be glad to teach you about their faith. Take a friend along if the step seems daunting, but go and learn and build relationships. Go to listen, to learn, and to understand, not to teach or to preach.

General cross-cultural training is a good preparatory step that will help smooth your adjustment to Almori culture. Numerous programs are available in dozens of locations around the world; check with sending organizations or those who have attended such training to find which is the most highly recommended in your region. At the time of this writing, I am not aware of any program that takes a "modified-mission" approach, such as has been discussed in this book, for describing your purpose and calling. They are either completely secular or they follow the traditional mission paradigm. Nevertheless, cross-cultural training is well worth the time and money.

If you are not yet qualified for your vocational identity, you will need to take steps to gain that qualification. If you can do so in Almoria itself you should seriously consider that possibility. We will discuss issues related to the life of a student in the next section, but going as a student may or may not be an option for you. In any case, relevant qualifications are obviously important for one's vocation.

LENGTH OF STAY, LANGUAGE, AND QUESTIONS OF CITIZENSHIP AND STUDENTHOOD

If you are called to move to Almoria, how long should you plan to stay there? The Apostle Paul, before his imprisonment, always moved on from a particular place of ministry in less than two years; Jesus' entire ministry fit into three. Today, many job contracts last for only two or three years, and there's something to be said for this duration. Knowing that an end is in sight in the relatively near future has a number of advantages. First, it can help you to keep your focus, because you know you will be leaving and so you will work hard to accomplish your purpose in that timeframe.

Second, it can help you to endure difficulties, and it may help you to give of yourself more freely because you know you will have a chance to recover once you return home at the end of your contract. It will also prevent you from "building your own kingdom," because you will not be around to enjoy it later. You will focus immediately on raising up others to continue what you begin.

On the other hand, a period of only a few years is insufficient for language and culture acquisition. Jesus and Paul faced no language or cultural barriers in their ministry, so they could launch into their work the moment they entered a place. Those of us who do face such barriers need at least two or three years to learn a language well, and learning a culture is a lifelong endeavor. Unless you devote yourself to mastering Almori before moving to Almoria, staying less than three years means your deeper friendships will only be with those who speak a language you already know. If you can find funding for an extended period of language study (whether in Almoria or elsewhere), you will reap dividends later if you are able to be disciplined in your study time and to immerse yourself in the Almori language.

Following on from duration of stay and language learning are questions of citizenship and life as a student. The greatest extent to which you can identify with the Almori people is by becoming an Almorian citizen yourself. This is not always possible, but it is an option that should be considered seriously. An intermediate option between visa-holder and citizen is that of permanent resident. A number of countries have a special category of permanent residency for retirees who want to spend their retirement years there, and in other countries permanent residency is available to anyone, regardless of age. Taking Almorian citizenship is clearly a commitment not everyone is called to make, but remember the early generations of missionaries who went out with no expectation of ever seeing home or family again. How many Western intercultural workers today go out with no prospect of returning?

Our context is different, one might argue. We do not live in the same world as those who went to Africa two hundred years ago with their belongings packed in coffins instead of in sea chests. That may be so, but the closest friendships and greatest impact come when we give of ourselves wholeheartedly and without reservation. People can tell when someone is just a sojourner, not a true resident. One can certainly give of oneself in Almoria without becoming a citizen; but for some, the formal commitment of citizenship helps foster emotional commitment to new friendships. Even those not called to become Almorian citizens can think of themselves as though they were seeking citizenship. Thinking as if you were—or about to be—a citizen helps you share in the concerns of those around you. As God told the Israelite exiles in Babylon, we too should "seek the peace and prosperity" of Almoria (Jer 29:7).

This verse, which precedes the well-known one that begins "For I know the plans I have for you" (Jer 29:11), appears in a passage set in the context of the exiles having to stay there long term, and of Babylon's peace and prosperity being linked to their own. It is not a passage calling for outreach to Babylonians. But it illustrates the fact that the mindset of a lifelong stay pushes you to pay attention to local concerns. By contrast, knowing that you will return home some day—however far off that day might be—gives you a completely different set of concerns from your Almorian friends, neighbors, and colleagues. They may be thinking about buying property, about long-term job security, about saving for their children's weddings. But you have none of these concerns—at least not with relation to Almoria.

You might object that thinking like a citizen conflicts with my earlier comments about being a guest, but it is definitely possible to maintain both the humility of a guest and the identification of a citizen. *Humility* means not assuming we know best about how Almorians should run their country; *identification* means making daily choices and setting daily priorities as if we were citizens—that is, living as people with a long-term stake in the outcome. Identification combined with humility drives us to interaction with Almorians who are seeking the best way forward for their country.

Another way to interact with Almorians interested in their country's future is as a student. But be a *real* student, not simply a student visa-holder. Being a bona fide student means more than just faithfully attending classes and fulfilling requirements. It means that the degree in question will play a real role in your career plans—a role that you can freely articulate to anyone who asks. It also must be in a subject which truly interests you. In other words, it is part of your vocation. Having a clear interest and a career goal for your studies gives you an answer for the times when Almorians will ask you why in the world you would want to study there, when all their students are trying to get to *your* country for their studies!

Note that being a student in Almoria may be a radically different experience from what you are used to at home. After having lived forty years in various cultures, I became a graduate student in the former Soviet Union. That was the greatest culture shock of my life—indeed, the only time I can really say that I experienced culture shock. The status of student there is so much lower than it is in the United States that even though I was treated well and was a graduate student not an undergraduate, just being among students as one of them was an entirely new experience for me. I also discovered that studying in a foreign language is an extremely challenging endeavor! All in all, although I passed the required philosophy course, was fascinated by the research, and learned a great deal, my student life is not an undertaking I will readily repeat.

STEPS FOR ACTION, REFLECTION, AND GROUP DISCUSSION

1. How has God used you in the past? What are your gifts, and what are you passionate about?
2. Where do you think God is calling you? Is your call based on relative need or on a more subjective sense of calling?
3. Who might be part of your support group? Pray for the right people. Also pray about joining a support group for someone else.

4. Find out if there is a place of worship near you, representing the faith of the people to whom you feel called. There will surely be some differences between those people and the ones near you; nevertheless, see what you can learn at the place of worship near you about their faith. Listen, learn, and seek to understand. If the people you are called to are predominantly atheist, seek to learn about their worldview and its underlying philosophy.

5. Get cross-cultural training; even if you will minister within your "own" culture, remember that the wider culture is not the same as the evangelical subculture, so cross-cultural training is still relevant.

6. Get trained for your vocation, if you are not already. If you are called overseas, look into training options that may be available in the country to which you are called.

7. If you will be going overseas, pray about whether you will go for a few years or long-term, or even if you will seek citizenship in your country of service.

8. If you are called to a people who mostly live outside your country, have you considered the possibility that staying at home might give you the best opportunity to serve them? This may not often be the case, but it is always worth considering.

CHAPTER FOUR

FINANCES

Build shared vision and trust; have faith in God's provision.

We now turn to questions of funding: how much will it cost for you to live in Almoria? This matter is normally dealt with by a sending organization, so those choosing not to join one will need to determine costs independently. Expenses usually increase over time, not only because of inflation but also as one's family and life circumstances change. An important consideration with regard to costs—and relating also to your chosen identity—has to do with what standard of living you will adopt in Almoria.

How will you earn a living in your vocation? How will you cover any "extra" expenses you may incur (above and beyond those of a middle-class Almorian), such as for language study, children's education, and travel to and from home or for refreshment abroad to relieve the stresses of life in Almoria? What about your retirement? And beyond financial support (to anticipate what we will discuss in Chapter 5), how will you find the friendship, encouragement, mentoring, and accountability that you need in order to flourish?

The short answer to these questions is that you will need to trust God to provide. Our trust must always be in God. Yet God himself calls us to take steps to participate in his provision: "if a man will not work he shall not eat" (2 Thess 3:10). So without losing sight of God as our ultimate provider, and without becoming worried about how he will provide, we must take thought for our provision and make arrangements for it, knowing that this is God's plan.

GENERAL COMMENTS

Two basic options are available for funding: charitable and profit-based. In most cases it will be illegal to mix the two because the rules for charitable organizations in most countries preclude profit-making. Some likeminded investors might support your profit-making business because they believe in what you are doing and not because they think your business will be the best investment of their money from a profit-making perspective. Nevertheless, such an investment remains an investment, and not a contribution to a charitable organization.

The primary challenge in raising funds, whether for a charity or for a business, is one of shared vision and trust. Some donors may want a tax deduction for their contribution, which may not be possible if you are simply seeking a supplement to your salary so you can pay for travel home or for education for your children. But if your supporters trust you and understand the reasons for your chosen vocation and funding mechanisms, as well as why you cannot arrange a tax deduction for them, then they may be willing to forgo the tax deduction. In any case, if God is leading you, you can be sure your needs will be met.

THE TRADITIONAL
SENDING ORGANIZATION

For the past two centuries, the primary path for funding sent ones has been through a sending organization. Organizations have many benefits, such as:

- collaboration with others
- economy of scale
- provision of tax deduction
- financial and other accountability
- policies based on prior experience to prevent future problems
- sharing of resources to help tide workers through periods of lower-than-usual financial support

As I have already noted, few sending organizations have a mission statement that you could publicize in Almoria, but you may still want to be part of such an organization. The following paragraphs raise further issues to consider before you make that choice. I also mention a new kind of sending organization which *does* have a modified mission statement, before moving on to look at other options besides a sending organization.

Being part of a sending organization will most likely necessitate your participation in mission conferences and mission committees. As with membership in a typical sending organization, you would probably not tell Almorian friends or officials about your attendance at these gatherings. Perhaps this is not an issue, since these are isolated events and not part of a worker's normal daily life. Nevertheless, the problem of hidden identity can arise in these gatherings as well.

In favor of a sending organization, it needs to be said that being supported through a well-run organization is the best way to be free from financial worries when in Almoria. In some organizations, this is arranged through a pooling system that allows you to receive a steady monthly allowance even if your supporters are not keeping up a steady support stream. (When you next return home, you are required to bring your support level back up to 100% or more before you can go back to Almoria.) If you were never in danger of receiving a low level of support, the sharing of a pooling system may seem unfair; but for those with only just enough support, the pooling of funds can help avoid the constant stress of wondering whether or not you received enough donations to cover your expenses. This affords the freedom to focus time and energy in ways that seem most strategic, and not in monthly fundraising appeals.

Convenience and flexibility are not the only issues related to finances, however. If we are funded by donations from churches or other believers at home, what message does that send to those in Almoria who may join us in following Jesus? Do we want them to support themselves in the same way we do? This would only work for a small number who might be chosen as our co-workers and funded by additional contributions from our own supporters. Not only would this leave out other new followers of Jesus, but supporting even a select few in this way would serve to *strengthen* the existing Almorian perception (false though it may be) that Almoris are changing their religious allegiance for financial benefits. Furthermore, those receiving finances from abroad may be labeled as "foreign agents." From an Almorian perspective, working for an organization funded by Christians from overseas may appear to be easy and well-paying employment. Such a perception is not likely to have been what made *you* join your sending organization!

Incidentally, do not think that support-raising is more "spiritual" or requires a greater degree of faith than a "regular" job. God is our provider no matter what "source" he uses to channel his provision to us. Going overseas with full financial support requires faith in getting to the "100%" mark, and there will be times when support dips and requires replenishment. Getting a paying job overseas also requires faith. First, it often involves a short-term contract, and a great deal of faith is needed when one is "in between" contracts. Even the most lucrative job cannot tide you over an indefinite period of unemployment afterward, not to mention the problem of maintaining your visa status without having work. Also, arrangements for retirement and children's education will probably need to be made by you, unless you are blessed with a long-term employer who provides these benefits.

What if you like the idea of going without a sending organization, but you already have ties to one? You value those ties but you struggle with the fact that they need to be kept secret in Almoria. What should you do? Above all else, cry out to God for a solution. Bringing change to an organization is a long and difficult process, and you may have to settle for much less. It may come down to a choice between accepting the status quo and leaving the organization altogether. Between these two extremes—of departing abruptly on the one hand and resignedly accepting the way things are on the other—there are ways to transition out of an organization in a healthy manner. Leaving should not be sudden, and it should be based on God's direction as confirmed by others, not simply on your feelings. Sudden departures are unnecessary and can destroy relationships. Often it is possible to gradually move on without losing fellowship with former colleagues and friends. The problem of a hidden identity, no matter how strongly you feel about it, does not amount to a moral imperative for a sudden departure.

Leaving a sending organization may leave a hole in your finances. Donors who were happy to support you through the sending organization may be reluctant to give to you directly or through other channels. The financial aspect, then, may be another reason for a gradual departure: it allows time to replace the finances that came through the sending organization. Additionally, a gradual departure allows you to continue the relational connection with your donors and the associated accountability that often accompanies financial support.

After leaving, you may still want to maintain some level of association with your sending organization for relational reasons. In addition, there might be some amount of ongoing financial support available, in one form or another. You will have to decide whether such support would need to be hidden in Almoria, and if so, whether that would throw you right back to the hidden-identity approach with all its problems—which is why you left the sending organization in the first place. While it is best to move toward complete separation from an organization unless you are comfortable with Almorians learning of your affiliation, in reality the decision to separate completely may not be as simple as it sounds. There are always more options than just being "affiliated" or "unaffiliated."

Any form of affiliation with a missionary organization would need to be hidden in a highly restrictive country. You can be known as a member of an evangelistically outspoken home church and live in a highly restrictive country, but that is not true of membership in an evangelistically outspoken organization. The missionary organization is an altogether different entity from a church. That means you will have to choose: you can live with keeping your membership a secret, or you can live without membership.

If you have just left a traditional sending organization because it follows the hidden-identity approach, how can you compensate for the loss of helpful functions, such as recruiting and member care? An extreme solution would be to start an entirely new organization focused on restrictive contexts, but with an identity and purpose that completely match your identity and purpose in Almoria. There would then be no need for any secrets. Such an organization might be hard to fund, because most evangelicals would find it insufficiently evangelistic, and most other potential donors would be unhappy with any overt (or covert) evangelistic intent. It may also be challenging to find the necessary governance or sufficient management expertise.

Another solution could be to form a network. With links to the right people, not only mutual support but also recruiting and member care can be covered. It is all a question of finding the right contacts. In the long term, however, the lack of a formal structure, leader, or accountability system could make a network less reliable than an organization. A network depends entirely on relationships that must be continually nurtured in order for the network to thrive.

A third solution is to join an organization that provides services to intercultural workers, with a mission statement carefully crafted for today's restrictive contexts. Such organizations provide different types and combinations of services, from member care to financial oversight to management support. They can also take care of practical matters in place of your support group and they may even provide a channel for donations if your vocation is of a charitable nature. You can find an organization of this type by making inquiries within the intercultural outreach community.

One question remains, and it is applicable to any of these three options: are they just a new form of camouflage for the same old paradigm, or are they truly something new? In other words, do they simply provide better ways of hiding one's true purpose from the public gaze, or do they have a purpose that can in fact be shared with anyone? If a new form only provides better camouflage, it may still help to reduce the tension of a hidden identity; but if it truly represents a new paradigm, it can remove the need to have a hidden identity in the first place.

GETTING A PAYING JOB

An option other than joining an evangelical organization is to work for a completely non-religious entity. Many jobs are available overseas, and numerous resources exist for finding them, both on the internet and elsewhere. Having a paying job has its benefits, but it also comes with its own challenges. If you work for an international or government organization, or for a business, you will have to adapt to the priorities of that organization, no matter how much you thought you understood them before you accepted the job. An entity funded by any government, for example, will have political dynamics that you may not have anticipated. A business may focus solely on its profits to the detriment of its Almorian hosts. Some who work for large international organizations struggle with the failure of those organizations to do what is best for the local situation; instead, these organizations too often follow their own agenda. You may face specific prohibitions on mixing religion with work, intended to protect the organization or business as a truly secular entity. Once again, the purpose you have decided on after following the suggestions in Chapter 3 will serve you well, since it will be one you can share with anyone. "Anyone" includes not only the Almorian authorities but also your expatriate boss, so if you have worked out this purpose well you should have no problem sharing it.

Work in a non-religious entity may give you less flexibility with your time; however, your purpose in being there is not just for what you do outside of working hours. A "real" job provides natural relationships for witness and discipleship. David English of Global Opportunities has made a detailed study of the Apostle Paul's ministry and concludes that Paul never had regular financial support for his work (2013). Peter appears to have had such support, but Paul received only occasional contributions such as the gift from the Philippians (Phil 4:14–16). When Paul speaks of working "night and day" in 2 Thessalonians 3:8, English suggests that this refers to evening and morning, the cooler times of day when people worked: in other words, a full-time job. In 1 Corinthians 9, Paul lists a number of reasons why he prefers full-time work over "fully-supported ministry." These reasons include credibility for his message (v. 12) and identification with people (v. 22).

A word of caution for those with well-paying jobs or successful businesses: Jesus said, "Where your treasure is, there your heart will be also" (Matt 6:21; Luke 12:34). Having a high income is neither good nor bad in and of itself, but it can lead one to adopt a high standard of living as a default. The high standard of living is also not necessarily bad, but the question of standard of living is complex and should not be resolved by simply following what others are doing or what feels comfortable to us. Instead, we need to prayerfully seek wisdom from God and humbly seek advice from others, especially from others who come from a different background than our own.

Another work option is employment by an Almorian entity, whether government, nonprofit, or business. It might be a government hospital or medical school, or a private business offering English courses, for example. Local employment may not be economically feasible in poorer countries, and it may be less reliable over time than working for an international entity. Working for the Almorian government may also have legal ramifications in your home country. But if local employment does work out, its advantage is that the aims of your local employer are definitely "local" (although "local" may nevertheless not be in the best interests of the country's development).

STARTING A BUSINESS
OR NON-GOVERNMENTAL
ORGANIZATION (NGO)

If setting organizational priorities yourself is a primary consideration, your best option may be to start a business or NGO yourself. Naturally, doing so will come with its own set of challenges—an entire book could be written about different strategies for overcoming adverse government regulations, and the time and energy spent in obtaining permissions and visas. None of these challenges have prevented numerous expatriates—followers of Jesus or not—from starting businesses and NGOs in Almoria. But don't be under the illusion that this is an easy way to finance your vocation!

Business ventures must be real businesses, not just façades. That means first of all that real, experienced business people should be involved. Even if they themselves are not prepared to relocate to Almoria, they can take part in the venture (which may hire younger, less experienced workers) as a real business with real risk. Investment in such a business is not a donation, even if one chooses to look at potential losses as money contributed to a good cause. All those taking part in the business share some of the risk. Expatriates working in the business in Almoria should draw a salary that they can live on rather than receiving the majority of their support from a sending organization.

A portion of one's support, however, could come from a sending organization. Many people have more than one source of income, and it is unlikely—and perhaps unreasonable—to expect someone to cut off all additional sources of support besides income from their business. Nevertheless, if the salary drawn from the business is clearly no more than symbolic, then the motives of the "businessman" will surely be called into question by Almorians.

Furthermore, the business plan needs to be a real plan for a real investor. In other words, it is not enough for a venture to be funded simply because an investor shares your purpose of outreach to the Almoris; rather, the venture should be able to attract investors by its potential for profitability. You must genuinely desire to succeed in business—or, at the very least, to see the ones you are helping succeed—rather than simply seeking a way to be in Almoria for other purposes. Even if supporters at home are prepared to keep an otherwise unprofitable business going, sooner or later such an arrangement will result in problems of hidden identity. Almorians will eventually figure out if the business is real or just a front for something else.

Those not called to business but to NGO work should really do that work too. Avoid duplication by starting something no one else would do, or by going to a place where no one else would go. Prepare for the day when expatriates are no longer needed in the NGO and you will have to leave. The real needs of the project— rather than the desire to do other things outside of work or to remain longer in Almoria—should dictate work assignments and the comings and goings of expatriate staff. If you want to stay in Almoria beyond the time you were needed in the NGO, you should be able to find another job in the country. You may have to endure a spell of joblessness in Almoria and possibly even a period without a visa, when you are back in your home country between jobs.

Before you start an NGO, be prepared to divulge all the funding sources, and plan to have only one purpose statement and one set of core values. Having one public purpose and a separate private one that contains missionary language is yet another form of hidden identity. In funding your NGO, do not automatically rule out local resources available in Almoria, even if they may be less than you could get back home. Remember the five loaves and two fishes with which Jesus fed the multitudes (Matt 14; Mark 6; Luke 9)! It may not be advisable to use local funding for your own salary, because that would make it seem that you are in Almoria to receive and not give help, but Almorian staff salaries and other expenses can certainly come from local funding. You may need to scale down plans or increase timeframes in order to use local funding, but you can still be successful. As one friend commented, reliance on streams of donated funding creates an artificiality about what is started that will ultimately damage both what is created and its potential to lead to or contribute to healthy communities of Christ's followers.

Starting your own business or NGO is not the only way to have a say in the setting of priorities. If you can find the right one, joining a recent startup, or a locally run business or NGO in the midst of reorganization, can be as effective as starting your own—and far simpler. You may avoid most of the hassles of a startup yet still have a strong say in setting the priorities and ethos of the organization.

PAYING FOR THE "EXTRAS" OF EXPATRIATE LIFE

Many sent ones seek to live at a similar level to their Almorian friends, but because they are expatriates they inevitably have expenses that their local friends do not. First, there are trips to visit family and supporters, which may be considerably more expensive than their Almorian friends could afford. There may also be a need to make other trips, such as for international conferences or in between jobs, but remember that the more you travel, the farther you place yourself from most Almorians' experience. Even affluent Almorians may not travel much.

A second expense is connected with your health. Although you may have entrusted your health entirely to God when you went to Almoria, your status as an expatriate means that expatriate medical personnel in Almoria will feel morally obliged to care for you should you need their help. Even if you yourself do not seek their help, others will take you to them if things get serious. I have seen this happen numerous times. Yet even the best doctor cannot provide the required care if the facilities necessary are unavailable in Almoria. It is unfair to put medical personnel in the position of needing to provide care for which no infrastructure exists. This means that you will need to budget for medical evacuation insurance. It is relatively inexpensive, and it protects not only you but also the expatriate medical personnel in Almoria.

A third expense that all expatriates should plan for is saving for retirement. You may plan to retire in Almoria, but you never know how long you will be able to stay there. For this reason, you should definitely take thought for your possible return to and retirement in your country of origin. The principle here is similar to the one behind the purchase of medical evacuation insurance. You may have entrusted your old age to God, but if you have nothing set aside for retirement, then those around you will end up having to care for you. God's provision most often happens through other people, but it is unfair to assume that they will always be happy to fill that role. So keep your trust in God, but make provision for your future. Any provision we make may fail, and at the end of the day our trust is in God; but to make no provision at all is simply irresponsible.

Another purpose for which extra funds can be useful is in money set aside to tide you over between jobs. Keeping any job long-term can be a challenge, but employment in Almoria is much more likely to be temporary than it is in your country of origin. Your employer may even terminate your contract early. This means that those wishing to stay longer than a few years need to continually be on the lookout for new jobs even while working.

Many more needs for extra funding could be mentioned. Perhaps you need a few years' full-time funding to study the Almori language. Or maybe you have ongoing expenses, such as for children's education or visits back home. Perhaps the adjustment to an Almorian standard of living is more than you can cope with and you need an additional living allowance. It is a mistake to advocate the same standard for everyone, because there are huge individual differences in how much a particular sacrifice "hurts" one person as compared to another. While a certain level of comfort may be more than sufficient for me, it may create real hardship for someone else, and I cannot consider myself better than my brother or sister just because I can live more simply. For me to sacrifice to the extent that they have, I might need to lower my standard of living much further still.

Rather than simply addressing ways of finding additional finances, however, I want to reiterate and expand on what I said earlier about standard of living. Although strong arguments can be made for a radical change of lifestyle to match that of the people among whom one works, experience shows that most sent ones do not manage it, especially if they have families. Other arguments are made about the necessity of living at a suitably high level if one is seeking to reach out to those who are well-off. The only thing that can be said conclusively is that standard of living is not a matter in which to blindly follow either our own inclinations or the patterns of the culture around us. Each of us must identify the level at which God wishes us to live. In doing so, we must be wary of simply adding a spiritual veneer to our own choices. We can avoid this mistake by considering the point of view of others—and this includes not only those others from a similar background as our own.

Whatever we conclude about the lifestyle to which God has called us, it may well require more money than an Almorian salary provides. So what can you do if you need extra funds? First, remember your trust is in God. When you have put your trust in him, return to the matter of your purpose and to those supporters who share that purpose. Presumably they trust you and there is sufficient accountability for them to be willing to contribute financially to your extra needs. They may wish to have a tax deduction for their contribution, and in this case a certain amount of "creativity" is indeed called for. In some cases, your funding may be able to come through an existing traditional sending organization, but we have seen that association with such an organization usually leads to a hidden identity in Almoria. In that case, it may be necessary to create a new nonprofit organization or to find one that has a less problematic identity. (As I have noted previously, such organizations do exist.) Here again it will be important to carefully and clearly define the purpose, such that legal and ethical requirements as well as issues of identity are all satisfied.

CONCLUDING THOUGHTS
ON FINANCES

Which is the best option for financing your vocation? No simple answer exists. The table below compares three broad options.

	FULL FINANCIAL SUPPORT FROM HOME COUNTRY DONORS	JOB OR BUSINESS WITH ALMORIAN COLLEAGUES AND CUSTOMERS	JOB OR BUSINESS WITH EXPATRIATE COLLEAGUES
USE OF TIME	Freedom	Constrained	Constrained, possibly heavily
TIME REQUIRED OUTSIDE OF ALMORIA	At least one month per year	Flexible	Probably frequent short trips
TRANSPARENCY OF FUNDING	Depends on how the funds come to you*	Yes	Yes
MODEL FOR NEW BELIEVERS	Questionable	Yes	Unlikely that Almorians can find such employment
NATURAL SITUATIONS TO LEARN ALMORI CULTURE AND INTERACT WITH ALMORI PEOPLE	Not naturally; such situations need to be sought out, perhaps with neighbors	Yes	Few

---

* If funds come via a traditional sending organization with a typical mission statement and publicity, transparency will rarely be possible. If funds come directly, or via an organization with a modified mission, transparency is possible.

	FULL FINANCIAL SUPPORT FROM HOME COUNTRY DONORS	JOB OR BUSINESS WITH ALMORIAN COLLEAGUES AND CUSTOMERS	JOB OR BUSINESS WITH EXPATRIATE COLLEAGUES
DEAL AT A DEEPER LEVEL WITH REALITIES OF ALMORI LIFE	Only if you create opportunities	Yes	Maybe not
SUFFICIENT FUNDING TO COVER ALL EXPENSES	Yes, but you have to raise the funds	Probably not	Probably yes

TABLE 1. Financial Options

In summary, Table 1 shows that 1) a job with expatriates is not likely to be the best option for interaction with Almori people; 2) a job with Almoris is the best for interaction but may not give freedom in use of time and probably will require supplemental funding; and 3) full financial support gives the greatest freedom in use of time but requires a new kind of organization to allow transparency of funding sources. Furthermore, full support sets one apart from Almori followers of Jesus, for whom such a livelihood is rarely an option. Even where it is an option, foreign funding for Almori believers serves to reinforce prejudice they may experience from other Almoris because their new faith is seen as nothing more than a way to benefit financially from wealthy foreigners.

Despite my arguments against it, I have to admit that the *easiest* way to finance your life in Almoria—notwithstanding the perceived difficulties of getting to the "100 percent" level—is likely to be donor support. A job or business might be more financially rewarding if it is successful and ongoing, but it probably requires more work than raising support. As I have argued before, however, "easiest" does not equate to "best" or "most effective." I do not mean to accuse fully supported workers of choosing second best; nevertheless, as comforting as financial security may be, it puts an expatriate farther than ever from the Almorians. It is all but impossible to identify with their concerns and perspectives from a position of comfort.

STEPS FOR ACTION, REFLECTION, AND GROUP DISCUSSION

1. What is your opinion about the value or necessity of a sending organization?
2. In what ways might finding and keeping a job in a restrictive country require more faith than raising support with a sending organization?
3. If you will be moving to a restrictive country, are there any job opportunities for you there? What are the advantages and disadvantages of each? Pray! Can you start an NGO, a business, or an educational institution? What would be the advantages and disadvantages of these options? Again, pray!
4. What extra expenses will you have beyond the basic cost of living? Will they necessitate a supplemental income?
5. What is the right living standard for you? How might your standard differ from others you will work with, and how will you manage that difference?
6. What do you think of the option of partial support, where one earns enough to live on but also receives supplemental income through a sending organization to cover extra expenses? Does this arrangement require a hidden identity just like full support does?

CHAPTER FIVE

SUPPORT GROUPS

The right support group makes all the difference.

Ongoing encouragement and accountability can be more difficult to find than financial support. And practical support is also needed. In this chapter we look at sources of practical, emotional, and spiritual support. Do not assume you need to look for support primarily from expatriates; an important source of such support, which is often overlooked, is the Almori friends you make or your Almori neighbors and colleagues. Finding support within Almori networks presents some challenges, one being the issue of patronage. I will discuss this, as well as issues related to two specific needs: support in finding suitable housing, and suitable arrangements for children's education.

SUPPORT NETWORKS IN ALMORIA

If you want a strong connection to Almori people, and not just to other expatriates working in Almoria, make sure that a significant portion of your practical and emotional support comes from Almoris and not only from foreigners. You can learn from the Almoris how to shop, how to get around, and what assumptions they make about life. This is easier said than done, and we will consider some implications of that difficulty in a moment. But difficulty does not change the fact that the people from whom you find day-to-day support are the ones who have the greatest influence on how you view Almoria and its challenges. The Almoris may not give you a more positive perspective than expatriates, but it will be a *local* perspective. Furthermore, your friendships with Almoris will be deeper if you are receiving from them and not just giving.

Bernard Adeney puts the matter of perspective in sharp relief:

> Many sojourners depend on friends from their own
> culture in learning the ropes of their new context.
> From the beginning they learn to see the new
> culture from the perspective of other foreigners.
> This reinforces the idea of their own perspective
> as an objective, neutral view of an unusual culture.
> The praxis of their initial orientation reinforces an
> alienated and/or paternalistic perspective. (1995:49)

Of course, there will be some things that only the expatriate
community can help you with, because they are probably the only
ones who can understand many of the challenges you face. But I
cannot overstress the value of keeping to a minimum the support
you get from the expatriate community and the time you spend in
the expatriate community.

If getting most of your support from expatriates will hinder you
from becoming rooted in Almoria, getting it from home will create
an even greater hindrance. This is not to suggest cutting off connections with your old friends, but rather opening up room in your life
for new ones. With Skype and other telecommunications services,
contact with people at home is limited only by the time difference.
Unlike in past decades, this means that your home church *can*
provide emotional and spiritual support when you are abroad, so
that your team in Almoria is not your only source of support. But
ongoing daily interaction with friends from your home country will
be yet another, and much more powerful, distraction from time
spent with Almori friends. Not only will it prevent you from getting
to know them and understanding their perspective, it will allow you
to effectively remain in your home country emotionally, making it
almost impossible for you to feel settled in your new home.

That said, you need to have practical, emotional, and spiritual
support from *someone*. The reality is that most expatriate followers
of Jesus, no matter how committed they are to having an Almori

support network, will get some of their support from expatriates and some of it from home as well. You will be surprised at how much support you can get from Almori friends, but there will still be times when you feel the need for a break from Almori culture. Some Western expatriates feel smothered by Almori hospitality, for example. Even those who obtain Almori citizenship will never be completely Almori. Some have chosen to immerse themselves fully in the Almori milieu, but from time to time they go somewhere else (usually to another city or even another country) to be with other expatriates and take a break from the demands and stresses of living in a different culture. An international church can also serve this function, as can external conferences.

Ideally, as much support as possible should come from Almoris with whom you use the Almori language to communicate, not another language you both may know. "But my Almori isn't fluent enough," you may object. Yes, it is difficult to communicate in a language you are just learning, but struggling to communicate is the only way to get into the culture. One of the best ways to learn Almori language and culture is to be part of a fellowship that uses the Almori language. Although you will understand little to begin with, you can focus part of your language study on the Scripture passages they are using.

The topic of language learning brings me to three points by way of an aside. Many good books and articles have been written on the topic of language learning, and I will not try to repeat or summarize those works. However, these three points bear repeated emphasis.

First, the purpose of learning Almori is to make Almori friends. To do so, you *must* use the Almori language at every opportunity. If you avoid situations in which you must actually use the Almori language, any language knowledge you acquire will remain useless. Since both learning and using take time, effective progress only comes when time is devoted to learning and practicing the language. Expatriates too easily find other activities for which they can use a language they already know, instead of Almori.

Second, an extended period of language study may well be the most challenging experience you ever face. When you go to another country where you do not know the language, you are forced to regress from being a competent adult to being like a helpless infant. This is a disconcerting experience, especially if you enjoy a sense of accomplishment! Numerous workers have been helped through this challenging period by a small book called *Isolation: A Place of Transformation in the Life of a Leader* by Shelley Trebesch. The author shows how times of seeming uselessness are in fact used by God to build relationship with him and strengthen one's capacity for service.

My third point is an elaboration of the first, with a caution. The best way to create opportunities for language use is to immerse yourself in an Almori community. That being said, a prerequisite to immersion is to find a trusted and experienced person, probably from outside your immersion community, who can monitor and mentor you as you learn the language and culture. This person can help you reach a balance between two extremes as you enter immersion. On the one hand, you might be tempted to withdraw into yourself because you are so far out of your comfort zone. On the other hand, you might overdo the immersion and burn out, give up, and go home. A mentor can also help you find healthy ways to deal with the loneliness that one often feels when surrounded by strange people. Loneliness may be an issue whether or not one lives in an Almori home, and whether or not one is single. For those who choose not to stay with an Almori family, "immersion" means following local norms for new arrivals—however intrusive they may seem from your cultural perspective. You may not end up in a place where the neighbors want to visit you the day you arrive (one of the more intrusive examples I have heard of), but learn what is expected of new neighbors in Almoria and do your best to fulfill it. Turn to your new neighbors for help in knowing what to do and how to do it.

Returning to the question of non-financial support, it is important to be part of a group whose members hold each other accountable in their walk with Christ. Include Almori friends in your accountability group, not just expatriates. It is, after all, the Almoris whom you have come to serve, and so *they* should be represented in your accountability structure as well.

In my experience, such inclusion of Almori friends is rare. First, there may not be any Almori believers to include. If there are, they may be outnumbered by expatriate believers and therefore unavailable to help you out. Or, in extremely restrictive places, meeting with expatriates may bring scrutiny from authorities that would endanger the lives of the Almori believers. On a more mundane level, being a part of your support group might not be the top priority on an Almori believer's list (and we are sadly misguided if we think it should be). Or the language and cultural barriers may appear insurmountable.

Beyond these obvious practical reasons, there is another, more troubling reason, though it is understandable and often justified: expatriates tend to trust other expatriates more than they trust Almoris. Including Almoris in one's accountability group means taking a step of faith that they will be trustworthy, and that communication will be effective despite the language and cultural barriers.

I have touched on some situations in which it may not be possible to meet with Almori believers. In such cases, you will have no choice but to meet with expatriate believers for fellowship and accountability. However, be careful not to give too much time to fellowship with expatriates, or you will have little time left for Almori friends.

Perhaps you have been called to a place where you do not know of a *single* follower of Jesus with whom you could have fellowship. It is not just a matter of language, it is a simple impossibility. In this situation, you need to pray for a team. Spiritual support is a *must*. It is not an optional extra. Service in Almoria is not something to be undertaken alone. No matter how eagerly you study the Bible on your own or how many sermons you listen to online, you will not survive spiritually unless you meet regularly with likeminded believers.

Therefore, pray for other workers to join you and form a team. Recruit some if you can. One way you might find others to partner with is via the website www.LinkingGlobalVoices.com, which provides links to various networks committed to global outreach of different types and for different parts of the world.

When you are communicating with others who may join you from outside Almoria, work hard to connect them with Almori people even before they arrive. Direct them to Almori contacts who can help them, rather than trying to help them yourself. Otherwise, you prevent your new teammates from enjoying the benefits of cultural immersion that were discussed earlier. You will not help anyone to be effective by making them dependent on you, and you may end up burning out yourself. This fact has to be carefully communicated over and over again ahead of time, because most new teammates automatically assume that you will be the one to provide most of their support.

One way to help set your new teammates' expectations straight is to avoid being a "middleman" in questions of placement and visa issuance before they arrive. Since you have nothing to keep private in arranging their placement, there is no reason not to give primary responsibility for the correspondence to those directly involved. You will naturally want to follow up and make sure that communication occurs in a timely manner, and you will want to be copied so that you can intervene to prevent catastrophic misunderstandings, but at all costs avoid doing all the correspondence yourself!

Not only should you connect new team members to Almoris, you should also strengthen your own relationships with Almoris. As your language skills improve, your interaction with Almori "supporters" can move from practical matters to deeper life questions. The more that you can gain an Almori perspective on life, the closer your friendships can become and the more fruitful your work in Almoria will be.

Damaris Zehner makes a strong argument against purely expatriate teams in her article "Building Teams, Building Walls" (2005).

Zehner describes her experience of an expatriate team that got in the way of its members' relationships with nationals, and says that a team uses up too much of a person's relational energy. While this is certainly not always the case, teams can easily become inwardly focused. They may spend so much time discussing their outreach that they are left with insufficient time to actually *do* anything. Zehner also points out that a team of expatriates easily excludes Almorians or gives them a lower status on the team. In other words, you will need an expatriate team if no other believers live in your location; but having formed the team, you will need to keep it outwardly focused. You should also prepare for the time when you will welcome Almori members.

Teams often experience conflict, and conflict is the number one reason for a permanent return home earlier than planned (English 2013). Working together closely with others can be difficult; friction occurs when personalities or priorities clash. Just as physical friction is eased by separating the parts that were touching, a team can decrease friction by giving space to its members. Although there are exceptions, the more closely that team members work together, the more likely they are to struggle with conflict. To use an analogy from sports, when intercultural teams function like a soccer or basketball team as opposed to a track team, the chances of friction are greater.

In a soccer or basketball team, even a superstar needs good teammates, both for defense and for "ball service." And if the defense lets the ball through or the service does not feed the ball to the superstar, the team loses. More balanced teams also require close teamwork and every player has to contribute. Every player also has to submit to the coach's game plan in order to succeed. In the context of intercultural work, these features of teamwork lead to conflict. Rarely is the leader of an intercultural team followed in the way that a good coach is. Instead, every member wants a say in every team decision.

Track teams, however, function quite differently because in each event except the relay race, team members compete individually.

This does not mean that they could achieve the same success without their team. Track team members spur each other on to greater achievement than any one of them could reach without the support and stimulation of the team. If a team wins a meet, it is the result of the sum of individual victories. Although winning a soccer or basketball game can also be thought of as a sum of individual victories, the nature of the sport means that even goal-scorers' achievements are reduced in value if the team loses, whereas a track team member's victory is undiminished by a team loss.

For intercultural work, conventional wisdom is that the soccer or basketball model is the one needed. And if the team functions well together, the result is indeed likely to be greater than the joint efforts of a track team. However, if tensions develop and cannot be resolved, it would be better to change the team dynamic to that of a track team rather than disbanding altogether. For more insights about teams of intercultural workers, read chapters 9–12 in *On Being a Missionary.*

SYSTEMS OF PATRONAGE AND THEIR IMPLICATIONS FOR ALMORIS IN YOUR SUPPORT GROUP

In many parts of the world, society functions through a system of patronage. In other words, those who have wealth and power ("patrons") provide protection and assistance to the less powerful (their "clients") in exchange for their service.[15] For example, a political leader in Almoria has considerable influence that he or she can wield in helping people find jobs. The political leader can also help people to avoid prosecution under the law. In societies with patronage systems, laws are often written for the benefit of the powerful, not the people. This imbalance means that those who

---

15. For an ongoing discussion of this topic see http://honorshame.com/to-be-or-not-to-be-a-patron/

lack influence need a patron to protect them from laws that allow other powerful people to take advantage of them. Benefiting from such patronage is not free, however. Strictly speaking, the cost is complete loyalty to the patron, though in practice the degree of loyalty required may be less than total.

This is relevant to our discussion about including Almori friends in your support system, because if you have a noticeably different income from your Almori friends, or significantly more or less power or prestige in the society, then the matter of patronage is going to affect your relationship with them—whether you like it or not. If you are wealthier than your Almori friends, there will probably be an unspoken expectation that you will act as their patron. You will be looked to as a provider. If, on the other hand, your status is lower than that of your Almori friend, there may be underlying expectations that you will do things for the friend in return for his patronage. Those of us from egalitarian societies may object to patronage systems, but they are the expected norm in many societies. Expatriates need to decide how to deal with patronage, both as potential patrons and potential clients.

If one chooses to reject the system of patronage altogether, there will be a number of likely outcomes. First, the people who were hoping to benefit from your patronage will be disappointed. They may be unaware that other countries have no system of patronage, so they will probably interpret your refusal to patronize them as a personal rejection or as downright stinginess. Such a lack of generosity, they would probably feel, contradicts your verbal message of Christian love. On the flip side, if you yourself lack a patron, you will face greater difficulty in accomplishing anything in Almoria, for a society that rests on patronage resists those who seek to circumvent the system.

On the other hand, trying to fit into the system of patronage can also be difficult. You do not know what is expected of either patrons or clients, and you may cause just as much disappointment by your mistakes in navigating the system as by an attempt to avoid it altogether. If you expect nothing at all for your largesse, you will be considered extremely generous or extremely foolish or both, and you may find that the other potential patrons whom you have "underbid" may not welcome your "stealing" their clients.

How then can an expatriate successfully navigate a patronage system? An adviser with insider knowledge is needed. Such a person should be a friend at about the same level of wealth and influence as you (in the *Almorian* context). As an equal, this person will not think of you as either patron or client and they can help you understand the expectations of patrons and of clients in Almoria. Perhaps you can also talk openly about the issue with your employer or sponsor in the country, and clarify as much as possible the expectations of both patron and client.

The idea of finding an Almori friend of equal wealth and influence came to me only as I was writing this book, and I admit I am not entirely happy with the way I have handled this matter of patronage in the past. My approach during my years overseas has been to avoid being a patron completely and to live as simply as possible. However, at times when my job made me an employer or when my wife and I employed someone for childcare, I was in the role of patron whether I liked it or not. I sought to hire the best person for the job regardless of religion. Often I also ended up in the role of client with those officials in charge of government departments for which our locally registered organization provided services. It was ultimately their goodwill that enabled the ongoing work of our organization and the resolution of various routine hassles. I also enjoyed a certain amount of patronage from some of my landlords. This was partly due to the friendly personal relationship we had with them, but with one exception the relationship remained that of tenant and landlord. In Almoria, however, even the landlord-tenant relationship often resembles "patron and client" more than "service provider and customer," which is more familiar to Westerners.

In conclusion, I strongly suggest that you do your best to find a suitable patron: someone with influence, but also someone with integrity. Also look for an Almori friend to guide you in navigating the paths of patronage. If you avoid patronage altogether, you will be at the mercy of every policeman or tax inspector who comes to your door. If you have a patron, however, you can contact your patron to help and advise you when such occasions arise. In any case, your trust is in God, not in your patron; but a patron can be helpful.

THE SPECIFIC NEED OF HOUSING

One of the needs for which you may be tempted to get expatriate help is housing. And not without reason: Almorians probably have little idea of what is important to you in a home. For North Americans particularly (and Westerners in general), a spotless toilet and bathroom are often a "must." Yet for most of the rest of the world, a toilet is dirty by definition, no matter how much effort goes into cleaning it, so it is usually left visibly dirty as well.

But it is not just the toilet that may be a challenge, and perseverance is called for in house-hunting. When Jill and Bob were looking for their first apartment in Almoria, they had trouble finding any acceptable place to rent in their price range. They were shown a dozen apartments that were considered perfectly acceptable for that price by Almorians, who all have their own ways to get their place ready to live in after renting it in rough condition. Jill and Bob, however, needed a place they could move into immediately. The thirteenth apartment they looked at would normally have been out of their price range, but the landlady (who owned a clothing store in a shopping center) had suffered a break-in and lost all her stock. She needed cash to begin again, so she dropped her price to meet Jill and Bob's budget when they agreed to a lump sum advance payment.

Certain deficiencies are more significant than others, such as the reliability of utilities: heat and water are especially significant. But how do the Almorians cope with utility cuts? Asking them what to do is more useful than asking fellow expatriates. In one city where we lived, the water would go off for multiple days at a time. Expatriates were often taken unawares and sought to solve the problem by keeping barrels of water in the house. The trouble with that is what happens to water that has been standing for a long time! But local residents usually knew in advance if the water was going to go off, and they would fill up their bathtub ahead of time. That water could then be used little by little for essential needs during the next few days. When we discovered this means of advance notice, we arranged for local friends to inform us each time they learned of an impending shut-off.

Learning from Almorians is more helpful for long-term adjustment than learning from fellow expatriates. Following the Almorians' suggestions may require lowering your standards, or you may need to pay more than you wished to reach your standards. You may need to find Almorians whose lifestyle is close to yours, to ask advice from; but as far as possible look for help from *Almorians*, not expatriates.

THE SPECIFIC NEED OF CHILDREN'S EDUCATION

Other than faithful, persistent prayer support, time well spent with one's children is surely the single most important factor in their wellbeing. This is just as true in Almoria as in your home country— if not more so. When I was growing up in Nepal, I went away to school at age six. I stayed with a family who had come to Nepal to run a hostel in the capital city of Kathmandu for expatriate children whose parents served in remote parts of the country where educational opportunities for their children were inadequate. My schooling through ninth grade was at an international school in Kathmandu. Until my own son was six years old, I never realized what I had missed by going off at that age (or what my *parents* had missed, for I myself had wanted to go to school in the city). When my brother and I were home on vacations, Mom stopped working at the hospital entirely and Dad took off half-days for a month, instead of the usual two weeks' vacation. He wanted to be available for us at least part of every day for that month. He was so available that we thought he had nothing better to do than play ball with us! It was only later that I learned how rare a blessing I had been given, or that I owed this blessing to a timely word from the wife of the mission director during our first year in Nepal.

Children's upbringing and education are the touchiest topics to address among sent ones.[16] My own childhood experience, combined with my children's experiences, encompasses every form of schooling for expatriate children, including local schools. Yet no amount of experience qualifies me to tell others how to bring up their child: each child is unique and each family is unique. The "right" way to raise our children is ingrained in us by our culture; no matter how much one may adapt to Almori culture in other matters, when it comes to raising children the culture of origin invariably asserts itself. This fact—to which I have seen no exceptions over twenty years—makes child-rearing an area in which conclusive or judgmental statements are particularly inappropriate.

Despite the danger of conclusive statements, some generalizations can be made. In thinking of the "best" education for our children, for example, we must be careful of uncritically adopting our culture's (or Almori culture's) assumptions. Rather, we need to

---

16. Resources abound for "third-culture kids" (TCKs)—children who grow up in the "third" culture of expatriates, which is neither their home culture nor that of the country where they live. Interaction International, CrossCulturalKid.org, and SHARE are helpful organizations. SHARE is focused specifically on education. The classic text on TCKs is *Third-Culture Kids: Growing up among Worlds* by David Pollock and Ruth Van Reken, and there are many other books available. One that deals well with the spiritual dynamics of growing up "between worlds" is called *Missionary Kids (MKs): Who They Are, Why They Are Who They Are, What Now?* by Rosalea Cameron (Queensland, Australia: Cypress Trust, 2006). Cameron herself grew up as an MK from Australia.

prepare them for whatever it is that *God* desires them to be.[17] That involves not only their academics, but also developing their other talents and nurturing their healthy development and their personal walk with God.

Fortunately, multiple options are usually available for schooling. The one least often considered is local schooling in Almoria, even though this option has the most potential for children's enculturation. Sometimes expatriate reluctance about local schooling has to do with different teaching methods; in other contexts there may be a concern about indoctrination into Almori worldview or religious beliefs. In still other contexts, an expatriate child may stand out so much as to create an unhealthy atmosphere, whether due to positive or negative attention. Sometimes the barriers have more to do with parents than with children. Experience shows that the parents' attitude toward a school situation has almost as much impact on the child's experience as the child's own feelings. In any case, Almori schooling does not work for everyone.

That leaves homeschooling, co-op schooling, online education, an international school, or a boarding school—or some combination of the above. All of these are valid options, as is local schooling. If you are the only expatriate in your location, then of course you have fewer options; but you may well find that someone from home is willing to come and tutor or teach your children.

Boarding school is the most maligned of all the options, probably because many sending agencies in the past required all their expatriate workers' children to attend boarding school from an early age. That was an unfortunate policy, geared more to freeing the parents for "mission work" than to meeting the needs of the children. Boarding school simply cannot provide the attention needed by most children, a fact that should not be underestimated. However, a mature, self-motivated child will often do well at boarding school, and the parting

---

17. I am indebted to David Huggett for these insights. His presentation at a retreat in 1995 has stayed with me ever since.

this necessitates is probably more difficult for the parents than for the child. The two and a half years I spent at boarding school in India, after finishing middle school in Nepal, remain among the best years of my life and I am grateful I had the opportunity to go there. But it is clearly not for everyone. Neither of my children was keen to go (and my wife even less so about sending them), and we had other options. In the end they did not go to boarding school, and they have no regrets about that decision.

STEPS FOR ACTION, REFLECTION AND GROUP DISCUSSION

1. Whether or not you are going overseas, and whether or not you join a sending organization, a network beyond your support group is helpful for effective outreach. Take steps to build the relationships needed to form a network. Depending on where you will be located, you may find an international church there—see http://micn.org. You may also find others with similar goals via geographical, ethnic, or vocational links at www.Linking-GlobalVoices.com. For most locations or people groups, however, the best way to find useful contacts is through a sending organization. They may not link you to their workers unless you join, but if you attend their conferences you may also be able to meet people connected to your place/people group of calling.
2. If you live overseas, what will it take for you to get a significant part of your spiritual and emotional support from nationals? What would keep you from that goal?
3. How can one set suitable limits on contact with friends and family at home?

4. What are the implications for language study if making friends in the language is the stated goal (as opposed to passing tests or reaching grammatical proficiency)? What are some ways to deal with the stresses of language learning, especially if it is not an area in which one is gifted? What are your thoughts (and feelings) about the immersion method of language and culture study?

5. Would you function better in a track-style team or a soccer/basketball-style team?

6. How do you think you would respond in a patron-client culture? In the West, patron-client culture generally gets a negative portrayal, such as in the movie *The Godfather* and its sequels. What aspect of patron-client culture conflicts with Western rules-based culture? If you do not find *The Godfather* objectionable for other reasons (such as its "R" rating), watch it with an eye to better understand the dynamics of patron-client culture, as well as to search for any positive elements of this culture that may be observable under the overall negative portrayal of the film.

7. What is God's best for our children, as distinct from what our culture says is best?

Theological and Conceptual Foundation

CHAPTER SIX

KEY CONCEPTS THAT LED TO THE HIDDEN-IDENTITY APPROACH

*God's mission is more likely to be compromised by methodology
that falls short of God's way of doing things than by a
government that does not allow missionaries.*

The hidden-identity approach did not arise in a vacuum. Rather, it began in a particular historical context and worldview. Within that framework, it was the only logical response to the restrictions placed on intercultural workers by an increasing number of countries. With the benefit of hindsight, however, we can reevaluate the historical factors and worldview.

FOUR HISTORICAL LEGACIES

The church of today has been shaped by the many centuries during which Christians held decisive political power in their nations. This history can tempt followers of Jesus today to understand the kingdom of God as territorial rule of a "Christian kingdom" (or "Christendom"). But the Greek word translated as *kingdom* in most English versions also means *reign*. Just as Jesus' first followers mistook his teaching on the kingdom for a promise of earthly rule (Acts 1:6), his followers in succeeding centuries have also confused the reign of God in individual hearts with the reign of Christianity in a particular territory.

Even though Christendom has long ceased to exist as a political reality, its continued presence as a concept in millions of minds adds an unhelpful geopolitical element to intercultural outreach today. And not just today. According to mission historian Dana Robert, "What was good for Christian fortunes in the Roman Empire [after Emperor Constantine identified himself as a Christian] was bad for them in Persia, Rome's chief rival." Intervention on their behalf by the powerful Roman government only worsened their situation: "Sponsorship by Rome meant that Christians in Persia appeared to be enemies of the state." When Constantine sent a letter to the Shah of Persia seeking better treatment of Christians, the Shah instead responded with increased persecution (Robert 2009:18). This dynamic is as much at play in the twenty-first century as it was in the fourth. The West, or America, has taken the place of Rome, and Almoria the place of Persia.

Douglas John Hall, author of *The End of Christendom and the Future of Christianity*, suggests that the key problem with a Christendom mentality is that power, not love, is seen as the means of change:

> Briefly put, it is my belief that the Christian movement can have a very significant future—a responsible future that will be both faithful to the original vision of this movement and of immense service to our beleaguered world. But to have *that* future, we Christians must stop trying to have the kind of future that nearly sixteen centuries of official Christianity in the Western world have conditioned us to covet. That coveted future is what I mean when I use the term 'Christendom'— which means literally the dominion or sovereignty of the Christian religion. Today Christendom, so understood, is in its death throes, and the question we all have to ask ourselves is whether we can get over regarding this as a catastrophe and begin to experience it as a doorway—albeit a narrow one— into a future that is more in keeping with what our Lord first had in mind when he called disciples to accompany him on his mission to redeem the world through love, not power. (1995:ix)

In other words, the very idea of Christendom leads us in the wrong direction. Whether or not rulers in the past were right to make

Christianity their official religion, we today are wrong to wish for political domination by Christianity. This is not to say we should avoid politics. Quite the contrary. We should participate, and not close ourselves off from leadership roles. Being salt and light requires participation in society. This participation means that some followers of Jesus will find themselves in positions of authority, and their identity as followers of Jesus should shape the way they exercise their offices. But a longing for political domination by Christianity is misplaced. Only when Christ returns will he be proclaimed Lord in all the fullness of that title. In the meantime, he calls us blessed when we are meek, poor, and persecuted—not when we rule. He calls us great when we serve, not when we lord it over others.

The second historical legacy that affects our current mindset is that of colonialism. Colonial rule was bolstered by a belief in the colonizers' right—and more than that, in their *duty*—to rule their colonies, allegedly for the benefit and improvement of the colonized people.[18] Today, the "duty to rule" has been replaced by a sense of duty to educate. The impulse behind this education, as well as "democratization" and "development," is similar to the one behind the "civilizing" mission of colonialism. It is the notion that *we* know best, and that we are duty bound to help others to reach our advanced level. The campaign for human rights also falls into this category. Great effort is expended by Western governments and non-governmental organizations in promoting these values. The fact that Western governments promote them does not make free elections or human rights wrong or bad—far from it! But when good things are pushed on you by rich and powerful foreigners they look less like a blessing and more like an imposition.

No wonder, then, that many of the supposedly benighted Almorians resent our help and advice, even if they agree that they

---

18. Concerning the supposedly altruistic motives for colonialism, many of the agents of colonial rule were in fact motivated by a desire to improve the lot of the colonized peoples, even if many others had no such intention and simply used the fine words as a mask for the economic motives of such rule.

have a need. This is all the more true if they feel there are "strings" attached to assistance, such as a mandatory evangelistic message addressed to all recipients of an aid shipment (or to recipients of free medical or dental care). When we give assistance, is it yet another form of domination (in that it creates dependency), or is it in fact servanthood? The line is a fine one. How many of us have a "hidden colonialist" in us? Even when we have life-saving knowledge, if we blurt it out without taking time to listen to those who we believe need that knowledge, is that domination (forcing our views on others) or servanthood?

The colonialist legacy also can lead intercultural workers to assume that it is our right and duty to be in Almoria doing what we feel called to do there. And yes, if God has indeed called us, God can make a way for us. The trouble comes when we begin to feel that the Almorian government owes us a visa for as long as we want one. Thus, if we are denied easy entry, we feel justified in finding ways around the obstacles whether or not those ways are in accordance with the intent of Almorian visa regulations. We forget that being a guest in Almoria is always a privilege, not a right.

Today's sending organizations are a further legacy of the colonial period, but they deserve separate mention because the hidden-identity approach is a product of the modern sending organization. Also, the roots of the sending organization go back much farther than the colonial period. Some mission historians argue that the roots go back to the setting aside of Paul and Barnabas in Antioch (Acts 13:1–3), the first time that a church sent anyone to do outreach. While a two-man team certainly cannot be considered an organization, the setting apart and special sending that occurred in Antioch are what a sending organization is designed to facilitate. Other historians find the roots of the sending organization in the Christian religious orders of the Middle Ages. Strictly speaking, these began in the twelfth century with the Cistercian order; but they follow a legacy going back to St. Benedict in the sixth century and beyond him to the earliest days of Christianity.

The first modern sending organization was the Baptist Missionary Society, founded in 1792 and followed three years later by the interdenominational London Missionary Society. Dozens of other such organizations were founded in the succeeding decades, and to this day sending organizations follow the same basic model. They rely on financial support from churches and individuals, and their workers raise the bulk of this support when on home assignment. Almost exclusively, those supporting the work view these workers as missionaries, regardless of what the workers may call themselves or how successful they may be at getting supporters to adopt new ways of describing them and their work.

Two things have changed in today's world that make it difficult for the modern sending organization. The independence of former colonies means that no foreign government can directly set the agenda in those countries. In other words, even a powerful country can no longer guarantee entry of its missionaries into other countries. And what with Western cultural changes in the last fifty years, it is highly unlikely that a Western government would assist missionaries in *any* way, much less pressure a restrictive country to grant them visas.

In this hostile environment, in order to gain and maintain access to restrictive countries, sent ones chose to keep quiet about their organizational identity and funding sources when in Almoria: this is the hidden-identity approach. Given the background of Christendom and colonialism, and the assumed need to be part of a sending organization, this was the only logical choice and ways were found to justify the choice to those who felt it was deceptive or dishonest.

If we step back from Christendom, colonialism, and the status quo of sending organizations, the hidden-identity approach need *not* be the only choice. The modern sending organization, as a product of Christendom in the colonial period, is not necessarily suited to the post-colonial and post-Christendom world. Sent ones can look for entirely new ways to conceive of and engage in intercultural outreach instead of the hidden-identity approach. After more than thirty years of hidden identity, more and more sent ones in Almoria are doing just that.

Why has it taken so long to look for a new approach? Perhaps it is because intercultural workers from traditional sending organizations have generally fit into Almoria without any problem. They have worked in their non-religious vocations and have been welcomed for their dedicated service. They have succeeded, for the most part, in keeping their missionary identity hidden. In recent years, however, two things have changed. First, numerous governments are becoming increasingly restrictive, expelling some intercultural workers who had been there ten or twenty years. Second, many workers are discovering the costs to themselves and their relationships of having a hidden identity.

Another reason for the slowness in seeking new approaches may have to do with a fourth historical legacy that comes from a century-old dispute. Some liberal pastors and theologians at the turn of the twentieth century reacted against what they saw as an excessively other-worldly emphasis in many churches at the time. In response, these liberals proclaimed a "Social Gospel" that would transform society through biblical teachings. In doing so, many of them refused to preach at all about the need for personal salvation or about Christ's atonement for an individual's sin—despite the Bible's clear teachings on these subjects. For more conservative believers, however, the Bible's authority made it impossible to ignore individual salvation from sin. Because of the Social Gospel movement, conservative evangelical believers came to distrust any emphasis on doing good unless it was explicitly linked to a proclamation of Jesus' call to individual repentance for the forgiveness of sins. The division and distrust between these two groups of Christians has continued to this day.

The legacy of the Social Gospel controversy means that a would-be intercultural worker without a specific label of evangelist or church planter has to do a lot of explaining in order to be endorsed by an evangelical congregation. The continued suspicion of anything that is "just good works" has led us to *talk* more about evangelism and church planting than to actually *share* the gospel or start a church. In my observation, talking about evangelism and church planting or disciple-making has led to neither an increase in these activities nor to an increased effectiveness in doing them. What if, instead, we were to talk more about *loving* people than about evangelizing, discipling, or gathering them? Loving someone clearly includes a concern for their eternal well-being and closeness to God. Of course, talking about love may not generate any more love than talking about evangelism, disciple-making, or church planting has generated those actions. But talking about love never needs to be hidden from Almorian officials—and this is in stark contrast to talk about evangelism or church planting or disciple-making.

FALSE DICHOTOMY IN OUR WORLDVIEW:
MEANS AND ENDS, AND OTHER ETHICAL MATTERS

A lot of ink could be spilled discussing the relative importance of ends or means, but the fact is that the means are an inseparable part of the end. That is, they are an integral part of what happens rather than merely a path to that end result. A path, although distinct from a destination, is intimately connected to it. The experiences along the way are part of the trip. In the same way, our means of reaching a goal inevitably shape the end result. If Christian workers make a practice of being evasive, the people they influence will likely also become evasive. Or their evasiveness can have an adverse effect on their children, as we have seen earlier.

Stassen and Gushee suggest that in attempting to understand and implement ethics, analysis of "the variables that shape our ethics" is helpful (2003:68). The variables fall into one of four dimensions (see Fig. 1): our perceptions of reality ("way of seeing"), our thought processes about right and wrong ("way of reasoning"), our loyalties, and our basic convictions. Basic convictions are the deepest part of our way of seeing. Our actions flow out of who we are, which may not be the same as who we *say* we are or even *think* we are. Basic convictions are usually at a deeper level than our conscious, rational understanding of our ethics.

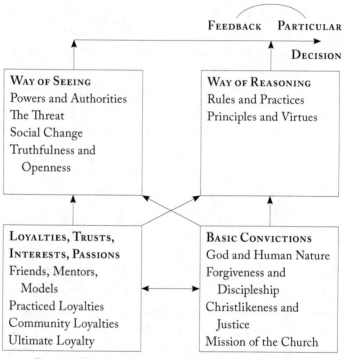

FIGURE I. The Four Dimensions of Holistic Character Ethics
(Fig. 3.1 from *Kingdom Ethics*, Stassen and Gushee 2003, p. 59. Used by permission.)

The four dimensions relate closely to the problem of hidden identity. Our basic convictions about Christlikeness, for example, are at the root of how we respond to government restrictions. Is it more Christlike to have no guile, or to give authorities answers that are almost cunning? Jesus told his disciples to be "as shrewd as snakes and as innocent as doves" (Matt 10:16), yet only Christ himself is the perfect combination of these two. Another aspect of Christlikeness is sacrifice: How willing are we to take a more difficult road in order to follow Jesus more closely? An authentic life is not necessarily an easy life.

Our *way of seeing* determines what we perceive as the threats to ourselves or to our mission. For example, we may see the Almorian authorities as a threat. But are the authorities the greatest threat, or is a methodology that relies on secrecy—or outright deception—a greater threat? God's mission is more likely to be compromised by a methodology that falls short of God's way of doing things than by a government that does not allow missionaries. So let us examine ourselves and ask the Lord if we are doing things the way he desires.

A further relevant question from the way of seeing is: What is our "desire for real understanding" (2003:67), our willingness to be corrected? In other words, if the hidden-identity approach has led us to be deceptive, do we have an open mind to hear that? Are we able to face reality and to be open to evidence that supports a perspective contrary to our own? Or do we always react defensively if our perceptions of reality are challenged?

Stassen and Gushee's third dimension is our *way of reasoning* about rules and practices, principles and virtues. All ways of reasoning begin with some assumed rules and principles—but what are they? Which dimension of right and wrong takes precedence? Is it politeness and honor, as in many Eastern cultures, or is it a code of right and wrong that must be followed regardless of the shame it might bring to others? Or is it simply a matter of being caught or not? Or even of "might makes right"? Followers of Jesus put the Bible at the beginning of their reasoning about ethics; but even there, different theological perspectives and different worldview frameworks lead to different prioritizations of the biblical material. This fact calls for what Adeney describes as "epistemological humility" (1995:188). None of us can claim to understand every verse in the Bible perfectly, so we would each do well to listen and understand before we seek to persuade others.

In going to cultures where completely different belief systems are at work, we need to learn the local way of reasoning about ethics, because this will be the framework within which we and our actions are *perceived*. Too often, we are so caught up with our own intentions and purposes that we become insensitive toward the *reaction* our activities are creating. Worse still, we tend to assume—incorrectly—that any negative reaction is directed at the good news, not at us or our method of presenting it.

Finally, Stassen and Gushee consider the impact of our loyalties, trusts, interests, and passions on our ethics. If a strict, literal following of our code would come at a cost to those whom we hold dear or to our goals and desires, should we follow our code or our loyalties and interests? What do we actually *do* when there is a tension or conflict between the two? In the case of the hidden-identity approach, do we bend our own code of honesty and openness for the sake of our interest in being in a particular place? If so, is that acceptable? In the reality of daily life, more actions will flow from our loyalties than from our principles.

Stassen and Gushee conclude: "It is far wiser to act with faithfulness to what is right, and let God control the outcome," than to base our decisions on what we think will achieve a good result (2003:167). I agree with them that the overall message of the Bible supports the importance of means, not just ends. God always wants us to do things in *his* way. In fact, the way we do something is part and parcel of the result. Jesus' life and teaching have led me to the conviction that the *way* the message is brought to people is in fact a big part of the message they receive. In other words, actions speak louder than words.

The challenge is to know what God's way is, particularly when our own culture and our own assumptions are bound up in our understanding of God and God's ways. We need humility because we have a limited ability to know and understand God's way. After doing our best to get it right we still need to be open to hear the perspectives of others. I include myself in this call for humility; readers of this book must decide for themselves, and I hope they will not judge harshly the decisions of others.

STEPS FOR ACTION, REFLECTION AND GROUP DISCUSSION

1. Reflect on your worldview. How has your thinking been influenced by Christendom? For example, does the phrase "Christian country" have a positive connotation for you? If so, does that connotation influence your picture of the ultimate aim in intercultural outreach? In what ways does that picture match—or not match—the biblical picture?

2. How has your worldview been influenced by colonialism? Have you adopted a "duty to educate" mentality toward other cultures? Or, in the opposite extreme, will you refrain from taking on leadership roles because that would involve having too much authority as an outsider? If one can combine the role of learner with that of teacher, and the role of servant with that of leader, a healthy balance can be reached.

3. When is assistance a form of domination?

4. If you agree that traditional sending organization mission statements and fundraising strategies lead inevitably to the hidden-identity approach, is there an organization that you could urge to change its mission statement and fundraising strategy such that no hidden identity would be needed?

5. Can sharing the gospel simply be part of who we are rather than an explicitly stated goal? Would removal of the explicitly stated goal of sharing the gospel affect the way followers of Jesus are received by others?

6. In the question of means vs. ends, has your obedience to the "what" of God's calling ever led you into questionable territory over obedience to the "how"? For example, do you agree with Stassen and Gushee that we must always use means that measure up to truthfulness in every sense of the word, since truth is a central aspect of God's character?

7. What do you consider to be the greatest threat to effective ministry in restrictive nations?

CHAPTER SEVEN

THEOLOGICAL FOUNDATIONS FOR A MODIFIED MISSION

Love never fails. (1 Cor 13:8)

Just as the hidden-identity approach arose in a particular historical context, it also is rooted in certain theological assumptions. In this chapter, we will look at some aspects of this theological context, and I will suggest changes that I believe could lead to a healthier approach. The chapter challenges two commonly held—though perhaps not commonly acknowledged—assumptions.

Most of us would not consciously claim responsibility for the fulfillment of God's purposes, but too often we behave as if that responsibility were ours. Likewise, few of us would assert that only certain gifts, vocations, or arenas of service are valuable; yet few of us actually place equal value on all gifts, vocations, or arenas of ministry. A healthy approach to outreach requires a balanced understanding of God's responsibility as contrasted to our own, as well as a sound regard for all gifts, vocations, and arenas of outreach.

RESPONSIBILITY, GOALS, AND MOTIVATION

To what extent is the fulfillment of God's purposes the responsibility of believers? Reformed Protestants at the turn of the nineteenth century held that God would "save the heathen" without human help and they were therefore skeptical about "using means" for reaching people with the gospel. The pendulum has swung to the opposite end in our day, and now we place too much emphasis on human means. Listen carefully to missions rhetoric and you could almost conclude that God's purposes will not be accomplished without our help. Although we do work together with God (Paul uses this phrase in

2 Corinthians 6:1), it is all too easy to forget who is the senior or managing partner in the relationship. It is also easy to place too much importance on the role of foreigners. Although at some point a foreigner or non-local person does need to go to any given group that has not heard of Jesus, most of those who actually follow Jesus in a particular place do so because a fellow citizen led them to faith. This is not to suggest that foreign workers are a waste of time and money, but simply to introduce a dose of humility to our self-importance.

Since God is the one responsible for completing the mission, our part in it must always be in accordance with God's means for accomplishing the task. Sometimes we may become so concerned about making an impact for the kingdom of God that we are tempted to use any means available, without thinking of the possible side effects. We might think that in doing so we are following the Apostle Paul's lead—"that by all possible means I might save some" (1 Cor 9:22)—but I believe that amounts to a faulty interpretation of this passage for a number of reasons. First, there is more than one way to translate the Greek word rendered "by all means." More importantly, one isolated verse does not override the clear biblical teaching that our methods, not just our results, should be pleasing to God. In other words, if the hidden-identity approach is not a method pleasing to God, then no goal, however lofty, can justify its use. First Corinthians 9:22, seen in context, is speaking about the sacrifices Paul is willing to make, not about ethical concerns he might be tempted to ignore.

We can also put too much emphasis on goals that we set for ourselves. Goals are good because they help us think about where we are headed. But they can also lead us to turn people into projects and dull our sensitivity to the Spirit's daily leading. And the current interest in objectives and mission statements comes not from the Bible but from the corporate world. That does not make them wrong, but in using them it is worth remembering that the word "goal" (or purpose, aim, etc.) in the New Testament almost always refers to holy living or to the ultimate goal of our faith: eternal life.

Perhaps our goal is to save as many individuals as possible today and we have taken on more responsibility for their salvation than God has intended. We may forget that each individual is a person of value, not just a number to be counted. Not all means are appropriate, and some may actually prove counterproductive. Or if our goal is to plant a church, we may be tempted to get it going no matter how the foundation is laid; but the ethical and relational foundation is of great importance.

When a church is begun without transparency or with a strong distinction between nationals and expatriates, this will surely lead to problems later—including conflicts or even a split. If our goal is phrased in terms of conquest, then once again there is a temptation to accept any method that successfully counters opposition tactics or strategy. If we make it our goal simply to walk in Jesus' steps, we may not have grand results to report back home, but we will have avoided many of the undesirable side effects just mentioned. And we will have accurately identified what our responsibility is: that is, to follow. A proper understanding of responsibility is important if one is to be committed to doing things God's way. Such an understanding also helps prevent us from setting goals that go beyond our mandate.

A word is also needed about the motivation for following Jesus to Almoria. I have not discussed motivation earlier in the book because I set out to address those who felt called by God to Almoria; their motivation was clear. Yet rarely, if ever, do we have perfect motivation for doing anything. If we understand our motivations we can take steps to change those which are not helpful. Change is needed, because our root motivation for fulfilling God's purposes makes a huge difference in the way we serve. Should we be motivated by guilt ("their blood will be on my head"), or by a promise of reward, or because we are simply tired of life at home and want an adventure abroad? Or should we be motivated by God's desire for all people to know him? Are we motivated by a desire to feel significant because we are engaged in important service, or are we simply moved by love of others?

Another factor to consider is whether the positive or the negative motivation is more effective; we must examine the implications of different motivations. Guilt may lead to a project-oriented mentality, which undervalues people. Reward might lead to counting stars in the crown, which overestimates our own importance. Only the motivation of love will never fail us. Love will guide us to the best response in every situation, whether we face opposition, government restrictions, or a lack of response from those who hear our message.

Many would argue—and correctly—that by far the most important expression of love is to seek the eternal salvation of others. Given this fact, we might be tempted to conclude that almost any means of "getting people saved" is acceptable because the terrible finality of eternity makes the end result the primary concern. The trouble with this approach is that the intended *recipients* of this love see the situation rather differently. They are likely to connect "love" to an interest in *their* concerns, however insignificant those may seem to the theologically correct evangelist. The evangelist, realizing this, may take an interest in the others' concerns, but if it is not a genuine interest it will be seen for what it is, and the message of salvation will have little chance of being heard. Thus, the "end result" of eternal salvation is best served by an approach that genuinely values individuals for who they are, not just for what they might become. God's way always values people for who they are; any other approach values people only as potential Christians.

EQUALITY OR HIERARCHY? A DISCUSSION OF GIFTS, ROLES, AND VOCATIONS

God uses us according to the gifts he gives us.[19] Romans 12:3–8 and 1 Corinthians 12:4–31 present a clear picture of the impor-

---

19. The present tense ("gives") is used intentionally here because of the many instances where people received a calling and only afterward found themselves equipped by God with the gifts needed to fulfill that calling.

tance of every gift. This is true for sent ones just as it is for other followers of Jesus. If all sent ones had only a certain subset of the gifts, how would the new believers being discipled learn to value other gifts? Unfortunately, people tend to "project" their gifts or their priorities onto others as being of greatest importance (Clinton and Clinton 1998:123). In other words, gifts other than evangelism, pastoring, and teaching are often downplayed in Christian writing and preaching and ministry. This may not be consciously intended, but it is difficult to value and develop in other people gifts you do not possess yourself. But the full variety of gifts is needed in a body of believers. Some gifts center on influencing or leading others through teaching God's word; others can be grouped around acts of service and still others demonstrate God's power (Clinton and Clinton 1998:125–26).

No hierarchy of gifts is supported by the Bible. The one mention Paul makes of "greater" gifts (1 Cor 12:31) comes immediately after his affirmation of all the gifts as important and cannot accurately be construed to support a hierarchy. Thus, if all the gifts are important, why are some gifts valued more than others by Jesus' followers? If people with a broad range of gifts may be called into intercultural service, not simply those with the allegedly more important gifts, then why do some followers of Jesus support a hierarchy of gifts?

Paul gives us the answer in 1 Corinthians 12:22–25, where he speaks about parts of the body that "seem to be weaker" (v. 22) and which are "less honorable" or "unpresentable" (v. 23). Despite Paul's assertion that the weaker parts are "indispensable" (v. 22) and the less honorable are treated "with special honor" and the unpresentable parts "with special modesty" (v. 23), the fact is that most people want to be strong, honorable, and presentable. Because we have put some gifts above others, the church suffers from a lack of the so-called "lesser" gifts.

In other words, "I don't have the gifts" does not necessarily say anything about my calling. God can and does give gifts in surprising ways.

A further difficulty arises from two types of confusion into which we easily fall. The first is to confuse a spiritual gift with an action expected of all believers. For example, all followers of Jesus must be prepared to tell others about him and what he has done for us (1 Pet 3:15), but not every follower is equally effective in doing so. Those with a gift for sharing the good news will see more results. Similarly, every believer is to care for others (Gal 6:9–10), but not everyone is gifted as a pastor. Comparisons like this could be made for all the gifts (Clinton and Clinton 1998:123). Every follower of Jesus is to live in a way that conforms to scriptural expectations, though not all are equally gifted in particular areas. We need each other, as 1 Corinthians 12 and Romans 12 affirm. Many believers would like to pass off all the tasks of the body onto their pastoral staff, rather than having the staff equip the members to do the tasks of the church. The Bible's pattern, however, is for every member to do "works of service" (Eph 4:11–12).

The second type of confusion is the kind that mistakes the gifts for the vocations (or roles) connected to those gifts. Someone with a gift of teaching God's word, for instance, may not necessarily be called to exercise that gift through a vocation of preaching to a congregation every Sunday morning. Such a person may be called to quite a different profession and seek other opportunities to exercise the gift of teaching. In the same way, not everyone with a gift for telling others about Jesus will be called to become a full-time evangelist as a profession.

The confusion with roles and vocations brings us to a second question: Does the Bible support a hierarchy of roles or vocations, even though it supports no such hierarchy of gifts? Biblical support can be mustered for both positive and negative answers to this question. Let us first look at some passages that appear to support a hierarchy of roles.

The Bible does give special honor to leaders in the church, whether they be teachers and preachers (1 Tim 5:17) or pastors (1 Thess 5:12–13). Jesus did set aside the Twelve as special Sent Ones (the meaning of the word *apostle*), and Paul and Barnabas were specially set aside for their ministry by the church at Antioch (Acts 13:2). In Acts and the Epistles, more attention is given to the work of spreading the good news of Jesus and starting churches than to the exercise of other gifts. Furthermore, whether we like it or not, human societies—and the churches within them—do end up with hierarchies. This sociological fact is not a supporting argument for hierarchies, but it does help to explain their existence quite apart from supporting arguments.

In order to evaluate the arguments in favor of hierarchy, we need to first look at the biblical arguments *against* a hierarchy of roles or vocations. First, Jesus himself taught that no believer should have a special title or position (Matt 23:1–12). While one might argue that Jesus' teaching there was aimed more at the attitude required of leaders than at the specific roles, his words do go against the notion of a hierarchy. And while the hierarchy I am speaking of is one of *emphasis* rather than of *status*, the two are almost impossible to separate in practice.

The trouble with a hierarchical view of callings is that we end up thinking "really holy people become missionaries, moderately holy people become pastors, and people who are not much use to God get a job" (Greene 2010:11). Kenneth Grubb, a strong supporter of intercultural outreach in the mid-twentieth century, put it this way: "We think of a special vocation, a separated caste, a peculiar body, whose duties are in some way different from those of ordinary every-day faithful Christian witnesses" (1931:5). A hierarchy of callings means that only those who follow the missionary or pastoral calling are given special recognition in the church. Instead, obedience to Christ should be celebrated whatever one's calling may be.

A moment's reflection shows that not everyone in the church will serve interculturally. "Everyone can give," it is said, and giving is indeed a blessing—more so than receiving, in fact (Acts 20:35). But giving money is no substitute for a life wholly dedicated to the Lord Jesus in every area, regardless of one's vocation. People with this kind of dedication should be honored in their churches no less than those whose dedication takes them across cultures. Otherwise church members will be hindered from having an effective outreach in their own workplaces. We can honor those who serve interculturally, but we should also seek models of commitment closer to home, which more people in our congregations could actually emulate.

This means we must avoid the assumption that planting churches is the "real" work of everyone called to intercultural service in places with few followers of Jesus. Yes, there is certainly room for those who focus on starting churches, especially among peoples for whom no church exists at all. But God is not limited to that service, and those whom he calls to another vocation are not engaged in an inferior or second-level activity. Many are simply called to be who they are, even if they are working as an engineer or nurse, in a place where Jesus' followers are few. It may be that they also have gifts and a calling to be church planters, and they will have to figure out how to do that. But church planting is not the only valid service, and those who "simply go" should not be looked down on as second-class believers. Rather, they should be given the same honor as any other followers who are engaging the culture around them in relevant ways and loving their neighbors as themselves.

A word of clarification is needed here. The point of the preceding paragraphs is not to suggest that there is no place for full-time ministers, whether they be pastors, evangelists, campus workers, or theologians. Few would question the validity of their ministry. Rather, the point is to validate the rest of us and to encourage the full-timers to double their efforts at equipping us. In doing so, they should work hard to affirm people for who they are and in the calling God has given them, rather than projecting certain gifts and vocations as being higher than others. The projection often occurs unconsciously, which is why pastors and teachers must be intentional about affirming *every* gift.

A further argument against a hierarchy of vocations is based on the fact that our work matters to God, no matter what it may be.

Two verses in Colossians 3 are often quoted in this connection: "Whatever you do, whether in word or deed, do it all in the name of the Lord Jesus" (v. 17), and "Whatever you do, work at it with all your heart, as working for the Lord, not for men" (v. 23). These verses are in the middle of a long section, 3:1 to 4:1, about what it means to live as one who has been "raised with Christ" (3:1). Colossians 3:23 is addressed specifically to slaves, who had no choice whatsoever about their occupation, but it applies as much to us no matter what lawful profession we may find ourselves in. The whole passage is focused on pleasing God whatever our station in life. The implication, then, is that we can please God regardless of what vocation we are called to. God is no more pleased by a pastor than he is by a plumber, if both are living daily as disciples of Jesus. This is just as true for those serving interculturally as for those who stay in their own culture.

Instructions about pleasing God in any walk of life are also found in 1 Peter 2:10–3:14. First Peter 2:12 explicitly links our behavior in daily life, whatever our calling, to God being glorified by those who see our behavior. The verse that follows these instructions for living tells us to be "prepared to give an answer" to those who ask about "the hope that [we] have" (1 Pet 3:15); and it is clear from the context that the reason people might ask us about the source of our hope is because of what they have seen in our lives. Again, this can be seen no matter what our profession. In fact, the less "spiritual" the profession, the more likely it is that people who see us do not yet know Jesus.

Finally, 1 Corinthians 7:20–24 exhorts individual believers to remain in the situation God has called them to (v. 24). Most of the chapter is talking about marriage and singleness, but verses 21–23 are about slaves. Although slaves are encouraged to gain their freedom if they can (v. 21), Paul's point is that a person's status in the world is of no consequence to God. A slave "is the Lord's freedman" and a free man "is Christ's slave" (v. 22). The key does not lie in our particular vocation but in the way we live our lives. A believer's daily life is important to God—every minute of it—whatever his or her profession may be.

Since every minute is important, we must not separate our day into a "spiritually unimportant" workday from 9 to 5 followed by a "ministry evening" from 5 to 9. This is not to say that every activity is of equal importance but that every activity can be done to the glory of God. Since our whole day from morning to night is for the glory of God, "ministry" is also all day long. It includes our family time as well as time spent outside the home. Nor is ministry only for those with a special vocation, set apart and above all others; it is for *all* vocations. Seong-Il Moon points out in his doctoral dissertation that ministry happens in four arenas, or as he puts it, "locations" of vocation: workplace, church, family, and community (2004:98). Which of these is most important? Says Moon: "Not only the church but also three other locations of ministry (i.e., home, local community, and the workplace) are valid places for Christian ministry" (2004:100–101). Again, this is just as true for a sent one in Almoria as it is for followers of Jesus in their home countries.

Concretely speaking, what does it mean that one "does ministry" at work? According to Moon, "All professional services in all locations can be equally valid ministries if they are performed fulfilling God's eternal purposes in a godly manner. There is no hierarchy of secular/sacred, religious/worldly, or ordained/lay" (2004:101). And not just "professional services"—family and community are also locations of ministry, offering plenty of opportunities for "non-professional" service. Those who do go out of the home to work need not start a Bible study there, nor share a particular gospel formulation with someone every day (which are suggestions one hears from time to time). Equally important is to love others and be a blessing to them. There will be opportunities to see God's transforming power, to exercise compassion, and to utilize other gifts, *as well as* to engage in those activities more commonly thought of as "ministry."

This is in contrast to the hierarchical view of vocation that existed in the medieval church and which has persisted to this day.

Moon challenges this hierarchy, pointing out that each follower of Christ is called to a unique combination of ministries in the different arenas. The key is to understand and obey one's calling, not to prioritize one arena over the others. Such a false prioritization can only lead to a false (and destructive) sense of guilt. In determining where and how to serve, Moon suggests that professionals "constantly respond to God's call with right motive, passion, and a right attitude toward various areas of service" (2004:101).

	GOVERMENT SECTOR	PRIVATE SECTOR	NONGOVERMENT SECTOR
INTERNATIONAL LEVEL	United Nations, World Trade Organization	Multinational corporations	Red Cross, FIFA, Lausanne Committee, Word Council of Churches
NATIONAL LEVEL	National government entities	Big business	National organizations
LOCAL LEVEL	Local government	Private individuals, small businesses	Grassroots organizations, churches

TABLE 2. Scope and Types of Professional Activity

Within the workplace arena, nine types of service are shown in Table 2. At the local, national or international level, one can work in business, government, or non-governmental organizations. Christ's followers can be found in each of these sectors; among expatriates in Almoria, these are the "accidental" sent ones mentioned in Chapter 2. By contrast, intentionally sent ones—those who go to Almoria with a sense of calling—work predominantly in the non-government sector at the local level. No doubt there are many reasons for this imbalance, but one of them is the tacit acceptance of the sacred-secular divide, by which we consider the other sectors less worthy of our participation. Far from being unworthy of us, these sectors present us with unparalleled opportunities. Not only do they provide a context for witness, but they also allow intentionally sent ones to work alongside "accidentally" sent ones and encourage them in their faith and outreach. Surely the relative absence of his followers in many of the nine sectors is not how Jesus would want it!

Jesus called us the salt of the earth (Matt 5:13). Salt, to be effective for preservation or for seasoning, must be evenly scattered throughout the dish. If all the salt is on one side of the meat or fish or pickle, the other side will still spoil. And if all the salt is on one side of the plate, neither side will be tasty. To be as effective as Jesus intended, let us be spread evenly throughout all the sectors of endeavor that make up our world.

Mark Greene, executive director of the London Institute for Contemporary Christianity, puts it well: "The key problem is not that we have failed to regard work as significant but that we have failed to regard all of life as significant" (2010:13). Francis Schaeffer had raised this matter in the early 1960s, calling believers to see the whole of life under Jesus' lordship, not limiting Jesus' lordship to "spiritual" life (Randall 2008:36). Greene develops this thought further, noting that we have left out "the kind of gritty engagement with daily life that you find in David's psalms, with his frequent references to the tools of his trade, his sense of God's intervention in his daily life as a soldier, songwriter, husband, adulterer, fugitive, father, general, king" (2010:13). It is worth quoting several paragraphs from Greene as he goes even further:

> SSD [the sacred-secular divide] makes people believe that art, music and the multifarious ways in which human beings express their God-given human creativity have no place in the kingdom of God—unless they have overtly biblical themes. . . .
> . . . [SSD] limits the apparent scope of [God's] concern to a very narrow band of activities, and thereby blinkers our vision of how wide and long and high and deep is his love. And how splendid he is. SSD makes us think that God is like a parent

who is only interested in one aspect of our lives, say, our academic performance. . . . They aren't interested in our love of tennis, or early medieval lute music, or *Scrubs*,[20] or our entrepreneurial ability to make money selling snacks bought at discount shops to our fellow pupils in school breaks. . . .

In fact, our Father in heaven is interested in all of our life. We see it in the beauty of the surroundings he created for Adam and Eve in Eden; we see it in his intense interest in what Adam would name the animals and the birds—such a mundane task, really; we see it in his tenderness as he makes clothes for his naked, rebellious children; we see it on every page of the Bible. (2010:15,17–18)

Greene's points are made even more emphatically by the Confession of Faith and Call to Action of the Third Lausanne Congress of 2010, held in Cape Town, South Africa:

The Bible shows us God's truth about human work as part of God's good purpose in creation. The Bible brings the whole of our working lives within the sphere of ministry, as we serve God in different callings. By contrast, the falsehood of a 'sacred-secular divide' has permeated the Church's thinking and action. This divide tells us that religious activity belongs to God, whereas other activity does not. Most Christians spend most of their time in work which they may think has little spiritual value (so-called secular work). But God is Lord of all of life. 'Whatever you do, work at it with all your heart, as working for the Lord, not for men,' said Paul, to slaves in the pagan workplace.

---

20. American TV show from 2001–2010.

In spite of the enormous evangelistic and trans-
formational opportunity of the workplace, where
adult Christians have most relationships with
non-Christians, few churches have the vision to
equip their people to seize this. We have failed to
regard work in itself as biblically and intrinsically
significant, as we have failed to bring the whole of
life under the Lordship of Christ.

A. We name this secular-sacred divide as a
major obstacle to the mobilization of all God's
people in the mission of God, and we call upon
Christians worldwide to reject its unbiblical
assumptions and resist its damaging effects. We
challenge the tendency to see ministry and mission
(local and cross-cultural) as being mainly the work
of church-paid ministers and missionaries, who are
a tiny percentage of the whole body of Christ.

B. We encourage all believers to accept and
affirm their own daily ministry and mission as
being wherever God has called them to work. We
challenge pastors and church leaders to support
people in such ministry – in the community and
in the workplace – 'to equip the saints for works
of service [ministry]' – in every part of their lives.
(Cape Town 2011:35–36)

I have argued against a hierarchy of gifts, and equally against
a hierarchy of roles or vocations. The quotes from Mark Greene
and Cape Town point to a third hierarchy that is common among
evangelicals. This ranking concerns the *actions* of believers, involving
what I believe is an unwarranted prioritization of some instructions
of the Bible over others. Kevin DeYoung and Greg Gilbert follow
this approach in their book *What is the* Mission *of the Church?* They
make a strong case for the primacy of disciple-making as the mission
of Jesus' followers, over against helping the marginalized or seeking

to change social structures (2011:26–27). The authors state their case graciously and they have included multiple references to the importance of concern for others, but these comments are qualified with warnings to be more concerned about the eternal suffering awaiting those who do not know Jesus than about any temporal troubles (2011:27).

DeYoung and Gilbert are correct to the extent that this present life does indeed pale when compared with eternity. Jesus himself gave singular importance to the preaching of a gospel of repentance and to the making of disciples—if nothing else, it was a key part of his final words to his followers. Nevertheless, I believe *the witness of the whole of Scripture speaks to the whole of life* and does not justify a particular prioritization of proclamation and disciple-making over other aspects of following Christ. Even if we would proclaim less and make fewer disciples without a prioritization of these activities (and I question whether that would be the case), the proclamation and disciple-making that does happen without prioritization is likely to be more genuine and to give less occasion to unbelievers for accusing us of hypocrisy or of simply seeking numbers.

Prioritization of some activities over others is a sufficiently important matter to warrant spelling out my point in more detail. I am contrasting two possibilities for prioritizing proclamation and disciple-making. The first option (DeYoung and Gilbert's choice) is to prioritize proclamation and disciple-making over other activities, with the caveat that it is important to practice what you preach. In other words, they *do* place value on other activities as well. The second option, which I advocate, is to prioritize *being* a disciple. This includes *all* of life, not just proclamation and disciple-making, though it certainly includes those activities also.

What is the difference between the two options? If one avoids prioritizing some activities over others, there might be less disciple-making and proclamation. There certainly would be less talk about it. There would also be less guilt carried around by those not as gifted in it. If one does prioritize proclamation and disciple-making, it may result in more of these activities being done. There may also be less focus on the other aspects of being a disciple. Emphasizing one aspect over others will rarely result in a good balance. Even if there has been a temporary imbalance in one direction, overemphasizing the areas that have been neglected will lead only to an imbalance in the opposite direction, not to a healthy balance.

I myself experienced an underlying sense of guilt and inadequacy for many years, because my service did not blossom in the areas of evangelism, pastoring, or even teaching. I thought that in order to be a worthy follower of Jesus, I should see fruit at least as a teacher. I don't know where I picked up such expectations, but they prevented me from developing in areas where I was gifted, since I was forever trying to be someone I was not created to be. When I learned to value *all* the gifts, I was freed from the false guilt I had carried. This does not mean I never teach, witness, or care for others—every follower of Jesus does these things. But in the lives of those more gifted in these areas, the fruit is more prominent.

In the secular world, authors Marcus Buckingham and Donald Clifton (2005) suggest that rather than spending all our energy trying to change our weaknesses (which we will continue to have no matter how much we try to eliminate them), we should instead focus on building our strengths, and find ways to compensate for weaknesses—for example, by working together with others who have the corresponding strength. This advice can be applied to the realm of spiritual gifts as well.

History bears out the fact that simply living one's life as a follower of Jesus can have a marked impact. From the very earliest days of the church when the Jerusalem believers were scattered, there have been "lay" people who went to other places bearing the news of Jesus and the testimony of his work in their lives. Andrew Walls provides an example from West Africa:

> I recall a survey of how the numerous congregations within one densely populated area of Nigeria had come into being. Time after time the seminal

figure was a new court clerk who was a Christian, or a worker on the new railway, or a tailor, carrying his sewing machine on his head, or some other trader. Some such stranger, or a group of strangers, had arrived and had started family prayers, stopped work on Sunday, and sang hymns instead, and some local people got interested. Or perhaps the initial impetus came from people from that village who had gone elsewhere—to school, to work, to trade, in more than one case to jail—and on return home sought the things they had found in their travels. The survey yielded no instance of a congregation founded by a missionary, and hardly one founded by any official agent of the church at all. In most cases the role of the mission had been to respond— sometimes, through straitened resources, belatedly and minimally—to an initiative within the community. (1996:87)

Not only Christians have followed this pattern. For example, Muslim merchants from Gujarat, India and "full-time" Sufi missionaries both played a key role in bringing Islam to Southeast Asia by the thirteenth century (Lapidus 1988:468–469). Few historical facts can be firmly established from this period given the dearth of written records. Historian Ira Lapidus draws the conclusion that there was "no single process or single source for the spread of Islam in Southeast Asia, but the travels of individual merchants and Sufis, the winning of apprentices and disciples, and the founding of schools, seems crucial" (1988:469). In other words, missionaries and non-missionaries appear to have complemented each other's efforts.

It may seem strange to end a chapter on Christian theological assumptions with an illustration from Islam. Yet the illustration serves a number of purposes. First, it never hurts to be reminded that we are not the only ones bearing an intercultural message intended for all peoples. Second, we are reminded that an effective movement combines a multiplicity of methods. And third, in our day of quarterly reports and bottom lines, the example from Southeast Asia reminds us that changes in faith and culture occur over centuries. Our desire to see results in our own lifetimes is understandable, but it belies the fact that God's timeframe far exceeds any single human life. When we keep God's timeframe in mind, we will be better able to keep a healthy balance in our theology as well as in our methods of outreach.

STEPS FOR ACTION, REFLECTION, AND GROUP DISCUSSION

1. Given that the current interest in objectives and mission statements comes not from the Bible but from the corporate world, how can we make use of these tools without being overly influenced by corporate values, which may conflict with biblical values?

2. What is your motivation for intercultural outreach? How can we make love our primary motivation? How can we balance the practical aspects of loving others with concern for their eternal salvation?

3. Have you experienced gift projection, in which a Christian leader (usually unintentionally) influences you to value his or her gifts more than your own? How can you transition to a healthy opinion of your gifts as well as those of others? Romans 12:3 directs us to think of ourselves with "sober judgment," in other words neither too negatively nor too positively.

4. How can we do better in honoring people whose lives are dedicated to Jesus, regardless of whether they have any special status in the church (such as the status of pastor or sent one)?

5. Which of the four arenas of ministry—workplace, church, family, and community—are the ones you are called to emphasize in your life? In other words, if you had to make a bar graph portraying your calling, how high would each of the four bars be?

6. Which sector of service are you in (see Table 2)? Is that the sector to which you are called? If not, what steps can you take to transition toward your calling? Do you agree that followers of Jesus should ideally be spread among all the sectors?

7. To what extent have you internalized the sacred-secular divide?

8. How can we ensure that *being* a disciple—with all that that entails—receives priority, rather than simply evangelism or disciple-making or good works?

9. What do you think about Buckingham and Clifton's idea of focusing on strengths rather than trying to get rid of weaknesses?

EPILOGUE

God works in spite of our mistakes. In fact, God may even prefer the mistakes of someone who is on fire and in motion over the "correct" theology and missiology of another who is lukewarm and sitting still. In writing this book, I needed to be reminded of this truth. Nevertheless, it is clear from Scripture that God does want us to grow up, to mature, to walk closely with him and do things his way. Once we have become aware of a mistake—whether it was made by us or by someone else—we should not repeat it, regardless of how much God accomplished in spite of it.

It is certainly easier to continue with the hidden-identity approach than to make any of the changes I have suggested in the preceding chapters. Full financial support from a sending organization takes care of everything, from pensions to college education funds. A team comes ready-made. But in Almoria a sending organization comes with a hidden identity, and we can do better than that. Yes, it will be a challenge, and we will need to step out in faith to trust God for things like a support group, job security, children's education, and retirement. Whether God calls us to become a citizen of the poorest country or to take a job in the largest multinational corporation, let us follow him and trust in his way.

God is a God of truth but that does not mean he condemns all shrewdness or never uses secrecy or strategy for his purposes. As George Verwer of Operation Mobilization says, God is about "messiology": God uses surprising methods to bring about his purposes, which more often than not "mess with" our categories and preconceived notions. In Verwer's words:

God in His patience, mercy, and passion to bring men and women to Himself often does great things in the midst of a mess. That is not an excuse for sin or failure; every Christian should strive to avoid making a mess. But it's the other side of the coin. It's God's way of working in spite of (actually, by means of!) the messes we make to bring about His plan and purposes. I sometimes refer to this as "radical grace." Large portions of Acts and the majority of the epistles demonstrate this. (2016:13-14)

In other words, any book like this one must be tempered with humility. Jesus is the master of the harvest, and I certainly cannot prescribe for him one method or another. Rather, when I see a fellow-laborer doing or saying something I disagree with, my first impulse should be to trust the master of the harvest to know what he is doing and to be in control. The master may ask me to speak to my brother—as I have done in this book—but I must do so gently and without judging, leaving all judgment to the master. There is a difference between raising an issue, as I have done, and passing judgment, which has not been my intention at all.

Having said that, I still believe secrecy too easily leads toward lying or to stinted or even broken relationships. Not that revealing everything about ourselves is good for relationships—we have seen that there is always a place for discretion—but my point is rather that we should avoid situations that would lead to a betrayal of trust. This truth transcends cultures, transcends multiple identities. We should order our lives in such a way that everything *could* be revealed if it were necessary or helpful to do so. We may not be able to rid ourselves of every secret, but we can certainly minimize them.

How can we make this change? For one thing, we can alter mission statements so that they can be stated in any context without fear. We will thereby avoid creating situations that must be hidden—or at the very least minimize what should be kept private. We need not be more specific in our purpose than to live as followers of Jesus in every part of our lives. This way of living brings freedom.

Opportunities to serve with an "acceptable" purpose—including the opportunity to speak when appropriate—abound all over the world today, allowing us to be complete disciples of Jesus in the process. Let us take advantage of these opportunities. It may require sacrifice, perhaps even a change of citizenship. But we will have no reason to fear if we trust the one who called us to mean what he said when he promised to give good things to those who ask him (Matt 7:9–11; Luke 11:11–13). Let us move forward with wisdom but not with fear, with humility but not timidity.

CONSULTATION ON MISSION LANGUAGE AND METAPHORS

Dear AD2-Announce Reader:

Please see the below Consultation Statement coming forth from the recent "Consultation on Mission Language and Metaphors" held at Fuller Seminary, 1–3 June 2000.

Let me encourage you to closely review this statement! As indicated therein, this is not a new issue—but the nature of our new technology, instantly releasing formal and informal communications around the world to an ever widening/deepening audience, calls for new reflection and an updated assessment of the language/metaphors used in mission communication releases. Thank you for your review, reflection and prayers!

That all may hear—soon!
Luis Bush
International Director
AD2000 & Beyond Movement

CONSULTATION ON MISSION
LANGUAGE AND METAPHORS
School of World Mission, Fuller Theological Seminary
June 1–3, 2000

STATEMENT:

We, the participants in the consultation, have gathered to think and pray together about the words, metaphors and images evangelicals use to communicate about the missionary mandate and endeavor.

As a relatively small group of mission agency and church leaders, theologians and communicators, we comprise neither a comprehensive nor adequately representative cross-section of the evangelical spectrum. We do, however, comprise a group unified in our concern that unwise language choices not be a hindrance to persons truly hearing the Gospel of Christ. We hope and pray that our tentative beginning here will encourage others in our context and around the world to grapple with some of the issues we have considered.

We regret that certain words and images long employed to call the church to mission have increasingly caused offense to the very people with whom we are seeking to share the Good News. Some of these words and images are biblical; some are motivational tools from the secular arena that we use to inspire involvement and action. Many are military in nature: "target," "conquer," "army," "crusade," "mobilize," "beachhead," "advance," "enemy," "battle."

We may know what such terms mean to us, but what do they mean to others? Are we unintentionally making those we most want to befriend feel we regard them as enemies, while helping opponents of Christian mission to make their case against us? Can we find more reconciling, redemptive words and images in Scripture and elsewhere that will aid us in expressing love, respect and effective witness for Christ, rather than creating an atmosphere of adversarial confrontation?

First, we agree about several basic principles:

1. We are not ashamed of the Gospel, which is salvation to those who believe. We seek to preach it, teach it, and demonstrate it through acts of love and mercy among all peoples in obedience to our Lord's command until He returns.

2. We realize that the Gospel itself is an offense and a stumbling block to those who reject it. We also understand that the mission of Christ will be opposed in many places and by all means.

3. We affirm that the Kingdom of God has triumphed over all the kingdoms and powers of this world at the cross. Nevertheless there is indeed a battle under way between the Kingdom of God and the Kingdom of Satan. In this spiritual battle we are privileged to partner with God in revealing Himself and setting the captives free.

While acknowledging these truths, we recognize the need to deal with several critical realities:

1. Metaphors and the mindsets and attitudes behind them are potent in shaping thought and compelling action. Positive metaphors are essential tools of missions and evangelism. When twisted or taken too far, however, they distort God's purposes. "Warfare" metaphors and terminology, while biblical in the cosmic/spiritual sense, have been misused in Christian mission communications. They have become increasingly counterproductive to mission work, sometimes endangering the lives of local believers, and are being used by opponents of the church to indict and impede its work. We therefore advocate an immediate end to the inappropriate use of such words.

    Yes, we are called to the discipline and single-mindedness of soldiers at war (2 Tim. 2:3–4). However, "our struggle is not against flesh and blood" but against the unseen rulers of spiritual darkness (Eph. 6:12). Jesus Christ fulfills God's age-old message of love, forgiveness, reconciliation and blessing for the peoples according to God's promise to Abraham (Gen. 12:2,3). Jesus Himself is the great master of redemptive metaphors (see His parables), and Scripture offers rich treasure of words and images we can use to call God's people to mission. He proclaimed good news to the poor, release for the prisoners, and sight for the blind (Lk. 4:18). We encourage Christian mission agencies and local churches to re-examine Scripture and restate their global task in terms consistent with the teaching and mission of Christ. Alternate words and images include blessing, healing, inviting, sowing and reaping, fishing, restoring family relationships, becoming reconcilers, peacemakers and ambassadors.

2. As a motivation for mission involvement, people are responding to the call to glorify God among the nations and wherever He is not yet being worshiped. They also respond to the call to follow Christ into servanthood and sacrifice, the call to lift up the downtrodden, the call to a life of great purpose and meaning in community with others of like mind. These are themes around which we need to develop metaphors to summon God's people to God's mission.

3. The new dynamics of globalization and instant global electronic information technologies are rapidly changing the context of our communication. The technology that opens the world to us also opens us—and our words— to the world. We can no longer maintain a dichotomy between what we say to the "home folks" and what we say to the world. The world, we must assume, will read or hear whatever we say to our own. Are we willing not to use language behind the back of unbelievers concerning their culture and location that we would not use face to face in sharing the message and love of Christ?

We encourage our evangelical friends, colleagues, churches and partner agencies around the world to think and pray with us about these things. We invite the reflection and wisdom of our brothers and sisters into what we hope will become an ongoing dialogue about these important issues, to the end that our light might shine brighter in the world, and that our ministry of reconciliation for the sake of God's great name might flourish.

End of STATEMENT

BIBLIOGRAPHY

AD2000 & Beyond Movement. 2000. Consultation on Mission Language and Metaphors. http://www.ad2000.org/re00620.htm, accessed January 14, 2014.

Adeney, Bernard T. 1995. *Strange Virtues: Ethics in a Multicultural World*. Downers Grove, IL: IVP.

Andrew, Brother. 1985. *Is Life So Dear? When Being Wrong is Right. Key Issues in Spiritual Warfare*. Nashville, TN: Thomas Nelson Publishers. (Rewritten and expanded from *The Ethics of Smuggling*, Wheaton, IL: Tyndale House, 1974.)

Andrew, Brother, with Verne Becker. 1998. *For the Love of My Brothers: Unforgettable Stories from God's Ambassador to the Suffering Church*. Minneapolis, MN: Bethany House Publishers. (Revised and expanded edition of *The Calling*, copyright 1996 by Open Doors Intl., Inc.)

Andrew, Brother, with John and Elizabeth Sherrill. 2001. *God's Smuggler. 35th Anniversary Edition*. Grand Rapids, MI: Chosen Books (a Division of Baker Book House). [original 1967]

Andrew, Brother, and Al Janssen. 2004. *Light Force: A Stirring Account of the Church Caught in the Middle East Crossfire*. Grand Rapids, MI: Fleming H. Revell.

———. 2007 *Secret Believers: What Happens When Muslims Believe in Christ*. Grand Rapids, MI: Fleming H. Revell.

Bok, Sissela. 1989a. *Secrets: On the Ethics of Concealment and Revelation* (Paperback). New York: Vintage Books.

———. 1989b. *A Strategy for Peace: Human Values and the Threat of War.* New York: Pantheon Books.

———. 1999. *Lying: Moral Choice in Public and Private Life.* 3rd ed. New York: Vintage Books.

Bonk, Jonathan J. 2001. *Missions and Money: Affluence as a Western Missionary Problem.* Maryknoll, NY: Orbis Books. [original 1991]

Buckingham, Marcus, and Donald O. Clifton. 2005. *Now, Discover Your Strengths: How to Develop Your Talents and Those of the People You Manage.* New York: Pocket Books.

Cameron, Rosalea. 2006. *Missionary Kids (MKs): Who They Are, Why They Are Who They Are, What Now.* Queensland, Australia: Cypress Trust.

Clinton, J. Robert, and Richard W. Clinton. 1995a. *Focused Lives.* Altadena, CA: Barnabas Publishers.

———. 1995b. *Strategic Concepts that Clarify a Focused Life.* Altadena, CA: Barnabas Publishers.

———. 1998. *Unlocking Your Giftedness: What Leaders Need to Know to Develop Themselves and Others.* Altadena, CA: Barnabas Publishers.

———. 2012. *The Making of a Leader, Second Edition: Recognizing the Lessons and Stages of Leadership Development.* Colorado Springs, CO: NavPress.

Daniels, Gene. 2005. *Searching for the Indigenous Church: A Missionary Pilgrimage.* Pasadena, CA: William Carey Library.

Danker, William J. 1971. *Profit for the Lord. Economic Activities in Moravian Missions and the Basel Mission Trading Company.* Grand Rapids, MI: Eerdmans.

DeYoung, Kevin, and Gregory D. Gilbert. 2011. *What is the Mission of the Church? Making Sense of Social Justice, Shalom, and the Great Commission.* Wheaton, IL: Crossway.

Dichter, Thomas W. 2003. *Despite Good Intentions: Why Development Assistance to the Third World Has Failed.* Amherst, MA: University of Massachusetts Press.

Elmer, Duane. 1993. *Cross-Cultural Conflict*. Downers Grove, IL: InterVarsity Press.

English, David. 2013. Tentmaking: Biblical and Global Basis. In *GO Equipped TENTmaking Course*. Pp. 2–5 of course materials.

Ernst, Carl W. 2003. *Following Muhammad: Rethinking Islam in the Contemporary World*. Chapel Hill, NC: The University of North Carolina Press.

Finley, Bob. 2010. *Reformation in Foreign Missions: A Call for Change in the Way Foreign Missionary Work is Carried on by Evangelical Christians*. Charlottesville, VA: Christian Aid Mission.

Freeman, Jon. 2010. The Dynamic Relationship Between Ethical Compromise and Ministry Effectiveness. In *Serving Jesus with Integrity: Ethics and Accountability in Mission*, Dwight P. Baker and Douglas Hayward, eds., 127–52. Pasadena, CA: William Carey Library.

Georges, Jayson. 2010. From Shame to Honor: A Theological Reading of Romans for Honor-Shame Contexts. In *Missiology: An International Review*, 38 (3): 295–307. Accessed online at http://mis.sagepub.com/content/38/3/295, October 31, 2013.

————. 2014. *The 3D Gospel: Ministry in Guilt, Shame, and Fear Cultures*. Self-published and Kindle Edition.

Gladstone, Rick. 2014. Tales Told Out of School in Pyongyang Cause Stir. In *The New York Times*, November 29, 2014. www.nytimes.com, accessed December 16, 2014.

Goldingay, John. 2003. *Old Testament Theology: Israel's Gospel Volume 1*. Downer's Grove, IL: IVP.

Greene, Mark. 2010. *The Great Divide*. London: The London Institute for Contemporary Christianity.

Grubb, Sir Kenneth G. 1931. *The Need for Non-Professional Missionaries*. London: World Dominion Press.

Hale, Thomas. 2007. *The Applied New Testament Commentary*. Colorado Springs, CO: David C. Cook.

Hale, Thomas, and Gene Daniels. 2012. *On Being a Missionary*. Rev. ed. Pasadena, CA: William Carey Library.

Hall, Douglas John. 1995. *The End of Christendom and the Future of Christianity*. Harrisburg, PA: Trinity Press International. (In the series *Christian Mission and Modern Culture*, Alan Neely, H. Wayne Pipkin, and Wilbert R. Shenk, eds.)

Hamilton, Don. 1987. *Tentmakers Speak: Practical Advice from Over 400 Missionary Tentmakers*. Duarte, CA: TMQ Research.

Harrison, Everett F. 1976. Romans. In *The Expositor's Bible Commentary, Vol. 10. Romans–Galatians*. Frank E. Gaebelein, gen. ed., 1–172. Grand Rapids, MI: Zondervan.

Jones, Juha. 2013. Private correspondence with the author, March 18, 2013.

Keller, Timothy W. 2001. The Need for a "Missional" Church. June 2001. Retrieved from http://download.redeemer.com/pdf/learn/resources/Missional_Church-Keller.pdf, July 6, 2013.

Keller, Timothy W., with Katherine Leary Alsdorf. 2012. *Every Good Endeavor: Connecting Your Work to God's Work*. New York: Dutton.

Lapidus, Ira M. 1988. *A History of Islamic Societies*. Cambridge, UK: Cambridge University Press.

The Lausanne Movement (The Third Lausanne Congress). 2011. *The Cape Town Commitment: A Confession of Faith and a Call for Action*. Peabody, MA: Hendrickson Publishers Marketing, LLC/Didasko Publishing.

Liefeld, Walter L. 1984. Luke. In *The Expositor's Bible Commentary, Vol. 8. Matthew, Mark, Luke*. Frank E. Gaebelein, gen. ed., 797–1059. Grand Rapids, MI: Zondervan.

Liu, Morgan Y. 2012. *Under Solomon's Throne: Uzbek Visions of Renewal in Osh*. Pittsburgh, PA: University of Pittsburgh Press.

Longenecker, Richard N. 1981. The Acts of the Apostles. In *The Expositor's Bible Commentary, Vol. 9. John–Acts*. Frank E. Gaebelein, gen. ed., 207–573. Grand Rapids, MI: Zondervan.

Love, Rick. 2008. Blessing the Nations in the 21st Century: A 3D Approach to Apostolic Ministry. In *International Journal of Frontier Missiology*, 25 (1): 31–37. Accessed on http://www.ricklove.net/wp-content/uploads/2010/04/Love_BlessingTheNations1.pdf, February 28, 2013.

———. n.d. Sheep, Snakes, and Doves. Accessed on http://www.ricklove.net/wp-content/uploads/2010/04/Sheep-snakes-and-doves-web-copy-_2_x.pdf, February 28, 2013.

Moffett, Samuel Hugh. 1992. *A History of Christianity in Asia. Volume I: Beginnings to 1500*. New York: HarperCollins.

Moon, Seong-Il Luke. 2004. *Toward a Missiology of the Missionary Professional with Special Reference to the Korean Church*. Ph.D. Dissertation, Fuller Theological Seminary School of Intercultural Studies.

Morris, Robert D. 1998. Shrewd Yet Innocent: Thoughts on Tentmaker Integrity. In *International Journal of Frontier Missiology*, 15 (1): 5–8.

Muck, Terry, and Frances S. Adeney. 2009. *Christianity Encountering World Religions: The Practice of Mission in the Twenty-First Century*. Grand Rapids, MI: Baker Academic.

Pollock, David C., and Ruth E. Van Reken. 2009. *Third-Culture Kids: Growing Up Among Worlds, Revised Edition*. Boston, MA: Nicholas Brealey Publishing.

Porter, Andrew. 2004. *Religion versus Empire? British Protestant Missionaries and Overseas Expansion, 1700–1914*. Manchester, UK: Manchester University Press.

Preston, Ronald. 1986. Lying. In *The Westminster Dictionary of Christian Ethics*. James F. Childress and John Macquarrie, eds., 363. Philadelphia, PA: Westminster Press.

Ramachandra, Vinoth. 2010. Mission in Face of Global Realities. Lecture at Fuller Theological Seminary, November 12, 2010. Report accessed November 26, 2010 at http://www.fuller.edu/About-Fuller/News-and-Events/News/Missiologist-Vinoth-Ramachandra-Speaks-at-Fuller.aspx

Randall, Ian. 2008. *Spiritual Revolution: The Story of OM*. Milton Keynes, UK: Authentic Media.

Rapley, Elizabeth. 2011. *The Lord as Their Portion: The Story of the Religious Orders and How They Shaped Our World*. Grand Rapids, MI: William B. Eerdmans.

Richards, Randolph E., and Brandon J. O'Brien. 2012. *Misreading Scripture with Western Eyes: Removing Cultural Blinders to Better Understand the Bible*. Downers Grove, IL: IVP.

Robert, Dana L. 2009. *Christian Mission: How Christianity Became a World Religion*. Chichester, UK: Wiley-Blackwell.

Roberts, Bob, Jr. 2007a. *Glocalization: How Followers of Jesus Engage a Flat World*. Grand Rapids, MI: Zondervan.

———. 2007b. We Aren't About Weekends." From www.christianvisionproject.com/2007/01/we_aren't_about_weekends.html, accessed April 1, 2012 by Larry Sharp, quoted in Oct 2012 article; not accessible Sept 2012.

Rowe, Michael. 1990. Soviet Baptists Engage in *Perestroika*. In *Religion in Communist Lands*, 18 (2): 184–87.

Sailhamer, John K. 1990. Genesis. In *The Expositor's Bible Commentary, Vol. 2. Genesis–Numbers*. Frank E. Gaebelein, gen. ed., 1–284. Grand Rapids, MI: Zondervan.

Sharp, Larry. 2012. Why I am NOT a Missionary. In *Evangelical Missions Quarterly*, 48 (4): 478–84.

Sidebotham, Bruce. 2001. Principle of Tolerable Risk Governs Ministry Opportunities. In *The Reveille Equipper* 5:2, March/April 2001. Published by MUP.

Solomon, Robert C. 1993. "What a Tangled Web: Deception and Self-Deception in Philosophy" in *Lying and Deception in Everyday Life*, Michael Lewis and Carolyn Saarni, eds. Pp. 30–58. New York/London: The Guilford Press.

Stassen, Glen H., and David P. Gushee. 2003. *Kingdom Ethics: Following Jesus in Contemporary Context*. Downers Grove, IL: IVP.

Strobel, Kyle. 2009. "Evangelical Idolatry." October 29, 2009. Retrieved from Theology Forum, July 6, 2013 4:18pm, https://theologyforum.wordpress.com/2009/10/29/evangelical-idolatry/#more-2833

Tenney, Merrill C. 1990. The Gospel of John. In *The Expositor's Bible Commentary. Vol 9 (John–Acts)*. Frank E. Gaebelein, gen. ed., 1–203. Grand Rapids, MI: Zondervan.

Tentmakers, Inc. 2010. What Is a Tentmaker? In *Worldwide Tentmakers*. http://www.worldwidetentmakers.com/education/what-is-a-tentmaker, accessed January 17, 2013.

Trebesch, Shelley G. 1997. *Isolation: A Place of Transformation in the Life of a Leader*. Altadena, CA: Barnabas Publishers.

Van Biema, David. 2003. Missionaries Under Cover. In *TIME*, June 30, 2003, 36–44.

Van Engen, Charles E. 1991. *God's Missionary People: Rethinking the Purpose of the Local Church*. Grand Rapids, MI: Baker Book House.

———. 1996. *Mission on the Way: Issues in Mission Theology*. Grand Rapids, MI: Baker Book House.

Verwer, George. 2016. *Messiology: The Mystery of How God Works Even When It Doesn't Make Sense to Us*. Chicago, IL: Moody Publishers.

Walls, Andrew F. 1996. *The Missionary Movement in Christian History: Studies in the Transmission of Faith*. Maryknoll, NY: Orbis Books.

———. 2002. *The Cross-Cultural Process in Christian History: Studies in the Transmission and Appropriation of Faith.* Maryknoll, NY: Orbis Books.

White, Tom. 2008. *Is Secret Christian Work "Illegal"?* (Pamphlet). Bartlesville, OK: The Voice of the Martyrs.

Wilson, J. Christy, Jr. 1980. *Today's Tentmakers: Self-support—An Alternative Model for Worldwide Witness.* Wheaton, IL: Tyndale House. (First printing 1979; current printing by Wipf and Stock, 2002).

———. 1981. *Afghanistan: The Forbidden Harvest. The Challenging Story of God's Work in a Resistant Land.* Elgin, IL: David C. Cook.

Wright, Christopher J. H. 2004. *Old Testament Ethics for the People of God.* Downers Grove, IL: IVP.

———. 2006. *The Mission of God: Unlocking the Bible's Grand Narrative.* Downers Grove, IL: IVP.

Zehner, Damaris. 2005. Building Teams, Building Walls. In *Evangelical Missions Quarterly*, 41 (3): 362–369.

INDEX